THE FUNDAMENTALS OF STUDENTS' UNIONISM

Z. E. Crispin

The Fundamentals of Students' Unionism
2017

LEAD EDITOR
David Westmacott

ISSUED BY
Selkirk College Students' Union
Room 0-127
301 Frank Beinder Way
Castlegar, BC VIN 4L3

ISBN-13: 978-1-975986-31-5
ISBN-10: 1-975986-31-8

CONTENTS

EDITOR'S NOTE

My first experiences with organizing were in the early 2000s when we brought the students of Okanagan University College into the Canadian Federation of Students. At the time, the BC Liberals were newly elected and had deregulated tuition fees. Compared to today, students were better engaged and organized, both on individual campuses and across the province. The fight put up against tuition fee deregulation was successful as a result.

Now more than any time in my involvement in the fight, we need competent organizers who understand the role of students in transforming society. The Canadian student movement is deeply fractured. Students in British Columbia pay roughly double the tuition that we did in 2001. These setbacks have mirrored similar troubles in the labour and other social movements, such as the intensified attack on the BC Teachers' Federation, the many dreary challenges of the Harper Government years, and the failures of the Occupy Movement worldwide. All this makes effective organizing more important.

When it comes to both expertise and vision, there should be no question that Zachary Crispin is the best person to put this book forward. I have had the pleasure of working with organizers from many backgrounds and political stripes, but few with a comparable record of efficacy and success. Over the years, he has organized campaigns that have saved students in British Columbia millions of dollars in foregone tuition fee increases. At the Selkirk College Students' Union he is a constant source of optimism and inspiration.

I am honoured to have a hand in this project. Looking over the various drafts, Zachary never accepted anything but the most rigorous scrutiny. Trying to get into the mind of organizers at other institutions, we worked together to present a clear "why" as much as an informative description of "how." It is my hope this book can be of some assistance to those brave enough to try to change the world.

David Westmacott

INTRODUCTION

Individually, students do not hold significant power in Canada. In order to achieve advancements – from cultural changes to political reform – students must work together. Solidarity and unity are the basis for collective action that can make students' political goals a reality. In order to build cohesion among students, organizers must work to break down divisions, educate students in large numbers, and spread the skills of political organizing.

This book was written at the behest of the Executive Committee of the Selkirk College Students' Union, and is meant to be a brief practical overview of college and university organizing in English-Canada. Selkirk College is a small institution far from the centers of power in this country, and the Students' Union relies on alliances with students elsewhere to achieve political goals. The Constitution of the Students' Union provides some insight into its motivations. Included in the Constitution are the following clauses, outlining the purpose of the organization:

PURPOSES OF THE UNION

a.   *Democratic Cooperation*

      The Union exists to organize students on a democratic, cooperative basis in advancing our own interests, and in advancing the interests of our community.

b.   *Information Sharing*

      The Union exists to provide a common framework within which students can communicate, exchange information, and share experience, skills, and ideas.

c.   *Political Reform*

      The Union exists to bring students together to discuss and co-operatively achieve necessary educational, administrative, and legislative change wherever decision-making affects students.

d.   *Service Provision*

      The Union exists to facilitate cooperation among students in organizing services which supplement the learning experience, provide for human needs, and which develop a sense of community with our peers and with other members of society.

e.   *Citizenship*

      The Union exists to articulate the desire of students to fulfill the duties and be accorded the rights of citizens in British Columbia, in Canada, and in the international community.

f.   *Student Unity*

      The Union exists to advance the interests of students by building a united student movement.

g.   *Universal, Accessible, High Quality Post-Secondary Education*

> *The Union exists to achieve the goal of a system of post-secondary education which is accessible to all, which is of high quality, and which is centrally planned; which recognizes the legitimacy of student representation and the validity of students' rights; and whose role in society is clearly recognized and appreciated.*

The Students' Union's policy documents reinforce these goals with the following declaration:

DECLARATION OF SELKIRK COLLEGE STUDENTS

PREAMBLE

The students of Selkirk College have a history of organizing for the betterment of Canada and the world. In the context of global outcry for action to prevent climate change, the worldwide aggression of colonial states, formal education becoming increasingly inaccessible, and the failures of capitalist democracy to address these and other issues, students seek an alternative. This alternative must respect the rights of nations to self-determination, address climate change effectively, and establish a democracy that fundamentally seeks to end exploitation on the basis of class.

STATEMENT

We the students of Selkirk College declare support for the following:

1.   *the right of all nations of the world to self-determination, including in Canada Indigenous nations, the Métis people, and Quebec;*

2.   *radical and fundamental changes to society to combat climate change, including vast reductions in environmentally damaging fossil fuel emissions;*

3.   *reshaping Canadian democracy, including constitutional amendments to recognise municipal government, establish a*

Both of the above statements were adopted by the general
membership of the Selkirk College Students' Union. Together, these
two documents represent the fundamental political reasoning behind
the organization's work. Self-determination for all nations in
Canada, robust and diffuse democracy, radical action to fight climate
change, and utterly universal education – maintained through a
society free from class exploitation; these goals are a profound
expression of humanity and of care for contemporary and future
generations. By adopting these positions, the students of Selkirk
College declare their commitment to a future when there is no fear
of the land or water being poisoned, when peoples can determine
their own fate free from colonial exploitation, and when the human
experience is not dictated by the power of those with great wealth.
The culmination of these aspirations is socialism and a critical
component in its success is the organizer.

These goals would require fundamental changes to the very basis of
society. In order to achieve them, the Students' Union engages in
political undertakings to develop students' consciousness, advocate
for reforms favourable to students, and advance the organization's
long-term goals. All short-term plans are part of a greater plan that
advances the long-term goals of the organization. Organizers are the
professionals and volunteers who work together to increase the
capacity of students to achieve their goals.

Selkirk College is a small institution and its few thousand students
are spread across eight campuses. In the context of a vast provincial
post-secondary system, the College is comparatively small. In order

for the students of Selkirk College to have any meaningful impact on social and political transformation they rely on the Selkirk College Students' Union. The Students' Union in turn relies on the solidarity of other student organizations working together to undertake political endeavors at a greater scale.

The student movement as a social movement exists to advance the interests of the student stratum of society. Given the vast proliferation of post-secondary institutions in North America, and globally, the post-secondary student has an increasingly important part to play in the transformation of society.

Students and Workers

The student movement does not exist in a vacuum. Other political movements have goals connected to universal public education, just as students are invested in the fight for other reforms. So long as there exists a class of wealthy individuals and corporations there will always be those who seek to privatize education for profit. Even partial privatization limits workers' participation and dilutes meritocracy at academic institutions. The struggle for universal education is by its nature a struggle of liberation for the working class.

Prominent among academics in the capitalist world is the tendency to promote petty individuality and personal importance. This tendency has existed throughout the history of post-secondary education for several reasons. In part because higher education was once an exclusive dominion of the very wealthy, and also because many historical streams of education promote the idea that more educated people have more value as people. In 1908, revolutionary leader Vladimir Lenin described liberal academics that wanted reforms as:

> ...the "opposition" of the bourgeois intellectuals who are concerned most of all to prove their loyalty, and who describe appeals to those in power as the political activity of liberalism.

Lenin is describing academics that do not view their role as emancipatory for the vast majority of people, but simply a tool of self-advancement. Self-interested politicking with no regard for the benefits to others is liberalism. The student movement can be a bastion of liberalism or it can ally itself with movements for workers' political power – the conflict between the two positions is the internal, ideological struggle on campus. As a force in class society, the student movement is at its best when it is a formidable auxiliary to the workers' movement for political power. In Canada, the vast majority of students grow up in working class homes, many work during their studies, and most will return to the wage-earning workforce upon completion of their education.

The wealthy have no need for the mass organization of students. The fight for free education means little to those who have no trouble paying high tuition fees. In Canada, the most significant gains of the student movement, from the Canada Student Loans Program to tuition fee freezes and reductions, have been achieved through a combination of the work of students' unions and labour unions. At many post-secondary institutions, labour union organizers were involved in the creation of the local students' union.

Building Collective Power

The broader concepts of student-worker solidarity and the role of the student movement are the topic of much literature. If there is a theme to this book, it is building collective power among students. All that students have to challenge those who oppose a more just society is their capacity for collective power and action.

In simple terms, organizers bring people together to take action toward a goal. However, organizing is not a simple, static process. Rarely do organizers simply gather a list of supporters, schedule a simple action, and end up with a campaign success. In order to achieve goals that fundamentally change society, organizers must build up the power of the movement.

Organizing starts small and local. It builds up through outreach and successful fights for reforms. By winning small reforms and showing larger groups of supporters that taking action can be successful, the organizer makes it possible to take on fights for more impactful reforms. The smallest subset of supporters is fellow organizers in a collective.

Building a collective may seem like a bit of a chicken-and-egg proposition, but like any undertaking there is an essential first step: articulating a purpose. Depending on the issue that will be addressed by the collective, organizers are likely already surrounded by potential comrades through class and social circles. With the purpose in mind, organizers start by initiating conversations about the issue. Where agreement and a desire for change are found, the conversation shifts toward gauging each person's appetite for taking action.

Many may find a goal desirable, but remain hesitant to take action because of a sense that the problem is far beyond them, or that doing something would require skills and talents they don't possess. Here the work of the organizer is to encourage and embolden supporters. This ability can be taught and developed. The methods and perspective contained in this book provide a framework for anyone to become an effective member of an organizing collective.

Making the shift from a shared vision of the future to an on-the-ground plan of action requires a significant, methodical effort. Organizing a collective means organizing people, and no two people see the same thing in exactly the same way. Each member of the collective will have their own perspective from concept to detail, as well as their own set of other obligations and barriers that will narrow the scope of their participation to something less than 100 percent of their time, resources, and focus. Getting to know comrades on a more personal level will help the collective to avoid significant misunderstandings, disruptions in the work, and clashes.

The strength of a collective can be measured in a number of ways, in output or maybe by sheer number of participants for example. However, this would be like judging a campaign strategy based on the quantity of buttons that are produced. The true measure of the strength of a collective is in its potential for impact and the shared dedication of participants to realize a compelling vision for the future.

Some organizing models limit their work to capacity of the organizers' collective, but this inevitably limits the success of the movement. For example, many students' unions are able to organize only as far as the personal contacts of board members and staff. This framework can never achieve the widespread and ongoing support necessary to challenge the powerful. Building collective power means scaling the work of a small local collective to match the unity and support for increased action. For example, if a single organizer brings together students in a successful campaign for extended campus library hours, but the campaign ends without developing the organizing skills of others or further mobilizing support for other student services, it can't be said to be a true success. However, if fighting for a simple reform, such as extended campus library hours, shows students that campaigning can be successful and develops the skills of local organizers, the movement is served.

Organizing is about connecting with people where they are socially, economically, and politically and empowering them to liberate themselves. Students' unionism is the movement for the social, economic, and political liberation of working people by organizing students. This book provides a broad overview of the technical knowledge needed for organizers in the student movement.

CAMPAIGN ORGANIZING

The term *campaign* does not mean the same thing for every organizer. For some a campaign refers to a single email sent out to a list, for others a campaign is an overall strategy to reach a political goal. Here the term campaign is used mostly in that latter sense, referring to an overall strategy with a coherent plan, logical steps, and a specific goal.

Campaigns are important for the campus organizer for many reasons. Without an over arching strategy it is difficult to keep a team or collective on the same page to reach any end. Creating campaign plans allow groups to democratically set out goals, and when they are well drafted they provide the basis for success metrics and timelines.

A forward thinking campus organizer must consider the impact and outcome of a successful – or unsuccessful – campaign as a part of the planning process. What will the impact of the campaign's message be on each of the organized groups on campus? Will the actions included in the plan be successful? What will be the political and financial cost of the effort?

As a note, from time to time various corporate terms and practices are mentioned in this book. While it is off putting to compare a campaign for free education to a business enterprise for petty profit, it is important to remember that capitalism's organizational tools are the most developed in the world, and thus should be harnessed in the interests of working people.

Criticism and self-criticism

The collective should evaluate tactics (evaluate all actions) against the strategies and goals of the campaign. The collective should not fear changing direction when it is what is going to be most effective. A good organizer can sort their ego from their ideas, and put forward thoughtful contributions to serve the collective's objectives. All ideas belong to the collective, and should be assessed on their merits. Criticism and self-criticism is the subject of a library of literature that is worthwhile for organizers to review.

Collective work

Whatever a collective is called, whether it's a political party cell on campus, a campaign committee of the students' union, or an independent group of students, the basis of the collective is the same. A collective with some level of permanency is essential to a campaign. Depending on the goals and strategy of the campaign, it may be appropriate to include instructors, campus staff, and other volunteers. Building the collective can be as simple as information tabling and posters in the halls. Always be sure to collect contact information from participants.

BUILDING CAMPAIGN MOMENTUM

Students do not take to the streets in protest, sit-in a politician's office, or hold a rally spontaneously. These actions, which have the potential to force decision makers to change when applied correctly, come as the result of organizing and mobilizing students. Just as the individual organizer comes from some less aware, emotional roots to grow into a fully informed and dynamic activist, so does the student population under the influence of proper political engagement.

Movement Building

Campaigns have a rhythm that reflects the development and orientation of the movement. As campaigns for small reforms succeed, participants and onlookers come to realize the benefit of collective action. It takes time for whole campuses of students to understand why they should support a cause.

When Quebec students went on strike in 2012, amassing some of the largest demonstrations in Canada's history, it wasn't the result of a short-term campaign. As early as 2010, tapped into and vigilant of the political discourse about the funding of education, groups such as Free Education Montreal and the Association pour une solidarité syndicale étudiante (ASSÉ) began informing students of proposed tuition fee increases. In large part, this included face-to-face conversation (linking access to education to the whole fabric of campus life), joining and establishing committees, working groups, and coalition relationships. It took years of work to build the student movement – to develop mass awareness and solidarity amongst students – in order to execute the mobilizations that ultimately prevented the proposed tuition fee increases from being successful.

Agitation

When an organizer stops someone on campus and says, "Would you like tuition fees to go down?" they're not engaging students on an intellectual level. Students will stop for the most part because they have some opinion on the matter that they will want to express. Some will stop because they've never considered the question, but the point stands. This interaction starts by the questioner invoking some superficial emotional response – agitating the person being questioned.

Agitation in campaign terms is the process of making these first engagements, as well as the ongoing tactics of agitation that keep volunteers returning to the campaign. This is a mostly emotional element of campaigning.

Education

Education is the process of transitioning the emotional response of agitation into both understanding and skill. There are several examples of campaign education that are common on campus, such as teach-ins, presentations, and guest speakers. Through the education component of a campaign or a collective's work, participants are elevated from activists to organizers.

Like agitation and organizing, education is an ongoing part of political action. For example, there is always more to learn about what makes strong education policy, how better to implement a campaign strategy, or what tactics work in what circumstances.

Organization and Mobilization

Organizing is the praxis, or actual implementation, of the knowledge and skills attained through education. Campaigns do not mobilize people on a simple and increasing basis. Student mobilization requires ongoing work to bring in the previously unengaged. Growing the capacity of new organizers to further the cause requires a training and development plan. There is no simple set of tasks to organize students, only strategies that are enforced by recurring organizational reflection, education, and action.

DRAFTING A CAMPAIGN PLAN

A common failing of the amateur organizer is to become hyper focused on the execution of an action, and not the goal that the action seeks to achieve. A proper plan helps organizers differentiate between tactics. Petitions, demonstrations, and shareable videos all have their place. Determine those tactics that will serve the strategy of the campaign.

Is the campaign plan going to be effective? Ask these questions as a group, and reflect on the contents of the plan:

1. What goals, immediate and long-term, are being served by the plan?

2.   Does the group have the human and financial resources to be successful?

3.   Which decision makers does the plan seek to influence, and will they be swayed by the campaign's actions?

4.   What power does the group have to leverage in effort to sway the target decision maker?

5.   Who is on the collective's side, and who will oppose the group?

6.   What concrete steps can be taken to achieve the campaign's goal?

7.   If the plan is unsuccessful, what will the next step be?

It is important to remain goal oriented when building and executing a campaign plan. One thing that tends to get lost in this work is planning for the least fun, most monotonous tasks. Data entry, such as typing petition emails into a spreadsheet, is exceptionally boring, but it is critical to campaign success. Make sure the campaign plan includes the most general, long-term goals, to the more minor, short-term tasks.

Components of a Campaign Plan

In the business world, a core technique of developing a business plan is to set a commonly understood vision for the company, a mission statement that outlines how the vision will be achieved, and a values statement that is reflected in day-to-day work. Student organizations, labour unions, and other political groups often employ a similar breakdown of ideas in campaign plans. For example, rather than Vision, Mission, and Values, the British Columbia Federation of Students has long trained activists to develop "Goals, Strategies, and Tactics."

In order to move through this process it is important to:

1.   collectively determine the goal of the campaign;

2.   ensure that the strategy of the campaign will achieve the goal; and,

3.   choose tactics that benefit the strategy.

GOALS

In the broadest sense, a goal is a determination of how the collective wishes things to be. Through participation and democracy, goals can be set to which the organizing group can adhere and be held accountable.

A good strategist will be able to propose a goal by taking into account the resources of the collective and the opportunities available to the group.

For example, tuition fees in British Columbia increased every year between 2005 and 2017. However, the annual increase was only about two percent. It is difficult to mobilize students to fight what they are easily convinced is a minor change in tuition fee rates. In 2016, when the BC Liberal government allowed post-secondary institutions to propose tuition fee increases of over $2,500 in some cases, students' unions were able to mobilize students to resist the increases. An opportunity had presented itself in the form of an aggressive blunder on the part of government, and students took that opportunity to build a campaign against the increases.

To borrow again from the business world, one way to determine if campaign goals are strong is to engage in a S.M.A.R.T. evaluation. S.M.A.R.T standing for Specific, Measurable, Achievable, Relevant, and Time-bound, is an evaluation of goals that was codified in a George T. Doran article published in November 1981 by the *Management Review*.

Specific:

When first sitting down to determine campaign goals, a collective may find that its members are diverse in their assessment of the necessary *immediate tasks* of a movement. It is important that a strategy serve a particular, specific goal. There can be intermediary goals that act as short-term benchmarks for a campaign, but those too should be specific.

Specificity can be determined by answering the What, Why, Who, When, and How of a campaigns goal.

Measurable:

When will the campaign have won? If the collective cannot answer this question, perhaps the goals are not yet measurable. Having measurable goals means that progress can be tracked. This also means the collective can measure the success of work, make adjustments, and boost moral among organizers and activists.

Achievable:

If it is Monday in North America, establishing socialism by Thursday afternoon is not an achievable goal – though it is certainly a measurable goal. Choosing achievable goals is about taking a realistic assessment of the various political interests involved.

The collective needs to have the people, money, and time to pull off the campaign.

Relevant:

Making sure the campaign is relevant is about harnessing opportunities. In the example mentioned above, tuition fee increases were about to put education out of reach for many students – an opportunity to mobilize those students to fight to stop the increases. Having a goal immediately relevant to those the group seeks to mobilize will greatly benefit the campaign.

Time-bound:

Establishing a timeline will allow the collective to critically reflect on the progress being made on the campaign.

STRATEGIES

Once the goals are determined, it is time to set out the particular set of events that need to take place for success.

Choose an Object

The object of a campaign is the person who is going to make the ultimate decision that will fulfill the goal. This could be a city official responsible for an important transit policy, it could be the Finance Committee chair of the college or university Board of Governors. The object need not be someone who is an enemy, they just need to have the power to make the changes the group is working for – it isn't about the object it is about the collective and those the group represents.

The Object is an Individual

Policy changes and large decisions usually fall to some form of committee, meaning many of the decisions made from on-campus government to federal government are made by groups, not individuals. However, these groups are usually led by an influential individual. Make the campaign work to influence the person who actually needs to make the decision.

Make the Object a Person

From time to time, organizers can over-focus on combating a culture or ideology expressed by institutions in a long-term sense. The collective may have a difficult time relating to particular people who have power. They may perceive them to make decisions only out of ambition, vanity, or loyalty to an opposing view. However, most individuals are also influenced by a sense of fairness, guilt, fear, and other emotions. These responses come into play when the object is personalized, and discussing this within the collective will help ensure all the relevant strategies are considered.

Secondary Objects

Secondary objects are individuals with influence on the primary object. The group will often have more access to the secondary object than the primary object. Trying to get funding from the students' union for a campaign but can't get a meeting with the Chairperson? Meet with a Director at-Large and ask them to bring it up. Campaigning to stop a tuition fee increase in the province? Meet with Ministry of Advanced Education staff if the Minister can't be reached.

Power Relationships

As the objects of the campaign are decision-makers, they have some power that the collective does not. However, no matter the object, some form of power exists within the campaign to influence that individual – if it didn't, every campaign would be a failure. It is critical to figure out what power the campaign has over objects and factoring that into the campaign plan.

TACTICS

Tactics are the tangible expenditure of campaign resources to serve the strategy. These are thought out and intentional actions with a foreseeable outcome that will advance the strategy. Tactics can vary greatly, with the intent to educate, agitate, mobilize, motivate, confront, and so on. The best tactics are those that simultaneously advanced the strategy of the campaign and develop the skill of volunteers and activists.

Brainstorming

The most effective tactics are those that stand up to the thorough scrutiny of peers. Ideas always start with an individual, and then should be vetted by the collective in the interest of being successful. In most settings, it is important to write down suggestions and ensure that everyone has a copy of clear notes (with the most notable exception being the consideration of illicit tactics). When it is time to come up with tactics sit down as a group, set a timeline, and have a fulsome discussion. Most often, it is best to let the group come together at a later time for final adoption of the plan.

Follow these guidelines when the group is discussing campaign ideas. Fostering a culture of open discussion will ultimately be a benefit to the campaign and the collective:

-       In a group setting, be clear that the ideas phase should allow every member of the collective to make suggestions without fear of judgment

-       Reiterate the goals, and allow the group to make creative suggestions about possible tactics

-       Foster a sense of inclusion by tossing a ball and allowing the catcher to say an idea, sitting in a circle and allowing each person to provide an idea in sequence, or some other method that encourages the quiet to participate

-       Connect ideas, allowing members of the collective to identify their suggestions in the end result

Spectrum of Tactics

The simplest form of political campaigning, and likely the oldest, is the conversation. Human beings have been turning to each other and griping about life for a long time. From face-to-face conversations, the spectrum of tactics gets more involved and complex. Letter writing mobilizes supporters to take an action with low commitment. Asking supporters to hand out leaflets will identify how many are willing to tell their peers they support the campaign. Demonstrations draw public attention to widespread concerns, and strikes actively disrupt economic activity. Each tactic plays a different part in a campaign. Organizers must determine which tactics serve the campaign strategy.

WORK ASSIGNMENTS

Assigning work in a collective is an important component of the execution of a campaign strategy. Even as a member of the collective vocally volunteers for a task, it should be clear and restated that the individual accepts an assignment of that work from the group. Once work is assigned, individuals should have the ideological fortitude to understand that this work is legitimate and important – that the work of a collective is a responsibility not just to oneself but also to the group as a whole. It is best if individuals can be assigned work for which they are both prepared and enthusiastic, but this is not always possible. Setting timelines and ensuring that members of the collective can report back on their progress will allow the group to assist those struggling to fulfill their assignments.

There is value in assigning work to each individual because it can instill a sense of personal investment in the success of the campaign. An imbalance in workload among organizers can lead to conflict.

There are tasks that nearly any individual can engage in to the benefit of almost any campaign. These tasks include:

- putting up posters, chalk graffiti, or other passive messaging;

- having face-to-face conversations with students;

- staffing information tables; and

- contacting lists via phone or email.

Organizers themselves should ideally be able to complete any tasks they assign to volunteers. Once assignments are made, organizers should be prepared to provide feedback and assistance. The more that a volunteer can gain from the experience, professionally, politically, and socially, the more likely they are to return.

Praxis and Patience

Activists and volunteers in any setting will quickly exhaust themselves if the demand for their time and type of work exceeds what they can commit to. This is sometimes colloquially referred to as "burn out." Burn out occurs when the various stressors and demands of participating in a campaign exceed the individual and collective benefit of participating.

Organizers sometimes interpret volunteers' faults as laziness, complacency, or apathy. Burn out is often blamed wholly on the participant. When the organizer or leader places blame on the volunteer for failure in the campaign, the goal is then forfeit. It is the responsibility of organizers to foster an environment that ensures that volunteers want to be a part of the campaign, even when it is in a difficult position or participants are uncomfortable.

While many factors determine supporters' participation in a campaign, organizers are not able to influence all of them. One of the critical components of building a movement to support the campaign is ensuring that there is the ideological fortitude amongst participants for them to determine and understand why they are taking action. It is the role of leaders in the collective and the campaign to inspire participants – a very real part of political work.

Practically, measuring the progress of a campaign committee can provide insight into the progress of ideological development and commitment amongst volunteers. Is attendance at committee meetings and events waxing or waning? What do regular students say about the campaign? Do they identify with the student movement?

Develop Volunteers

Students are critical, and sometimes cynical, about the value of political campaigns, but this does not mean they are apathetic about issues. Many of the students most affected by high tuition fees, those saddled with the highest student debt, are unable to commit to campaign work because the risk of failing a course or sacrificing paid work time is too great. Study stress, financial pressure, work, childcare, and family all make demands on students' time. This is not apathy, it is reality. Motivating campaign volunteers despite the factors that detract from participation is the role of the organizer.

Try New Things

Political campaigning is a process that might in some ways be compared to an armed conflict. Indeed, the term "campaign" is borrowed from the military world. Through the progress of an armed conflict, either side of opposing forces will develop tools to achieve a successful outcome, developing new approaches and weapons of war. Political campaigns also have a history of opposing forces developing new tools to counter each other.

Harnessing the creativity of the group can provide organizers with new tactics. These are most safely applied as innovations to long-standing tools and tactics – there is no need to reinvent the wheel for a campaign to be successful. Making carefully considered adjustments to existing tactics allows different people to input their skills and can keep the campaign ahead of opponents.

Psychological Ownership

In 2016, researchers from the Huazhong University of Science and Technology concluded that an employee's sense of psychological ownership over their work had a corresponding positive impact on their self-efficacy. This means that people who felt a sense of self in their work also felt more comfortable taking action and making critical decisions about their job.

> *"Psychological ownership and self-efficacy both had a significant positive influence on employees' proactive behavior, and employees' self-efficacy had a significant positive influence on their psychological ownership."*

Developing a sense of ownership for volunteers is part of passing the campaign on from solely the hands of the original core to a campaign committee or broader coalition. Acknowledging the input and hard work of participants can enamor those individuals. Ensuring that everyone has responsibilities in the campaign and receives follow up and feedback develops a sense of ownership.

Provide Historical Examples

Success draws volunteers, so it is important to be vocal about past victories. Illustrating how the action being proposed through a campaign has historically been successful promotes support for those strategies and tactics.

MESSAGING

A clear and focused message is critical to the success of a campaign. Messaging is the easy-to-follow story the campaign tells that makes a compelling case for the goals. Messages can vary based on audience, and be used to inform and encourage supporters and influence targets.

A study from the University of Wisconsin-Madison, developed through participatory research that placed graduate students within the activist community, suggests that robust media campaigns can arm the public with tools to vocalize existing ideas. This aids the campaign without requiring ideological conversion, campaign training, or moral appeal. In Wisconsin, English as an additional language communities confronted homophobia and transphobia by creating a simple message, focused on the concept that "Love is Love", that drew from real members of the community through print images.

> *"These encounters also effectively served to initiate dialogue with community members about how LGBT people were being perceived, what changes or improvements they wanted to see in their own communities, and how they hoped to enact them. Some of the staff members mentioned that these were conversations they had often found too difficult or thorny to initiate in the past, but that this project gave them language for beginning to tackle these issues within their youth groups and in the larger communities. This is a markedly different outcome than would be achieved from simply hanging the posters throughout the community without the component of facilitating personal conversations about the images."*

Simply put, campaigners in Wisconsin provided tools for volunteers to express what they already believed in order to inform their peers. While this example draws from a campaign not strictly contrived within the rest of this organizing framework, the example stands as a thoughtful message with a factual, focused, and compelling narrative.

When creating a message for a campaign, consider the following:

1. What *needs* to be said? Cutting out extraneous words will make the message more focused. Students are busy, and target decision-makers may be consuming messages from contradictory sources, so the more succinct the message, the more effective.

2. Connect the campaign's message to cultural references, trends, and memes, without making the connection seem silly or forced.

3. Review each word used in the message, and their alternative or slang definitions. Colloquial uses for words can make an otherwise serious message sound silly, unreasonable, or possibly offensive.

4. Express campaign messages in a way that is understandable, simple, and clear. Make the assumption that the viewer is learning about this issue only from the campaign message, and use common terms, acronyms, and phrases.

5. Avoid sarcasm, as it is usually impossible to determine inflection and tone in text.

6. Match the level of humour used in the campaign to the nature of the subject and the strategy of the campaign.

7. Make the issue local and relatable. Take the time to reduce regional, countrywide, or worldwide issues into community terms.

Making Use of Alternative Resources

Whatever the initiative, there are likely allies on campus from the outset of the campaign. Faculty associations, teaching assistant unions, support staff unions, students' unions, public interest research groups, women's centers, LGBT centers, and other campus groups may be able to provide in-kind resources. Asking for material assistance is also a way of opening up the discussion of greater support for the campaign by the assisting group.

AGITATION

For campus organizers, there are few interactions as important as the discussion in the hallway at an information table, or the brief interruption in the cafeteria. Speaking to students face-to-face is the single most effective way to bring awareness to an issue and ask for support for a campaign.

Some materials are common in this work on campus. The presentation of information at a table or in a handout is important. Describing the campaign and clearly highlighting issues and actions through visuals will ensure maximum participation. Make information tables clear, stand in front of them, and approach passers-by.

Informational Pamphlets and Leaflets

There was a time, when it wouldn't be unusual for newspapers to have circulation in the millions, that a political campaign could reasonably produce informational pamphlets with an extensive written thesis on an issue. That time has passed. While a thorough breakdown or essay on an issue addressed by the campaign might very well be useful for organizer development, it is not a digestible form of communication for passers-by.

Informational pamphlets and leaflets should support face-to-face conversation by providing a short written or graphical representation of the ideas being discussed. This information is best when available in such quantities that it can be given to those who wish to take it with them.

Other Materials

Pinning campaign materials to a backpack or jacket is a way for campaign participants to send a message to those around them that they support the initiative. Having a significant number of supporters wearing campaign material can lead to new support, as it will allow the campaign to connect with those often disconnected. Buttons are the most common form of this material, but other (often cheaper) alternatives exist, such as the squares of coloured felt used in Quebec student strikes.

T-shirts are a wearable material that helps supporters and others to identify volunteers, organizers, and committed campaign participants. While this material can be expensive for a small campaign, deploying t-shirts to the right people can mean a walking campaign billboard on campus.

Other types of materials to consider putting campaign messaging on:

Stickers	Postcards
Pens	Water Bottles
Note Books	Condoms
Door Hangers	

List Building

If someone supports the campaign, they will almost always give an organizer their contact information. Even without committing to take any action, providing contact information shows willingness to receive ongoing communication about the campaign. Collect contact information and follow up with every individual within 48 hours.

For an established organization, such as a students' union, having a living list of members and supporters is critical to the success of political initiatives. The Internet is by far the most universal vehicle for communication. It is the responsibility of organizers to be educated and engaged with common forms of online communication. Depending on the longevity of a campaign or collective, additional education about list building techniques should be pursued.

POLICY RESEARCH

Having a scientific, fact-based campaign requires research. Robust analysis of campaign goals and political issues, when deployed amongst supports, will ensure that organizers and participants are most able to combat opposition. Avoiding moralistic and emotional bases for political campaigns can ensure that organizers have a logical basis for advancing policy proposals. Decision-makers derive their power from systems and structures that largely ignore moralistic and emotional arguments.

Research need not be a complicated or overbearing process. If a campaign aims to change policy at a post-secondary institution, there is likely publicly available statistical information and research already available about the issue. Drawing from existing publications is the simplest form of campaign research.

Best Practices for Campaign Research

Information sharing is the basis for good research amongst campus activists. By sharing information between groups on- and off-campus, data can be brought to light that might be otherwise too fragmented for any one person to see the big picture.

1. Share any findings of campaign research and allow this information to be scrutinized. A second pair of eyes looking at the same information can reveal different impacts, outcomes, and opportunities.

2. Develop ways to present facts that are interesting and hold people's attention. Comparisons that both illustrate facts clearly and test the reader's values can add the power of persuasion to a campaign.

3. Use research and information tools already developed by allies or easily adapted from those fighting for the same thing elsewhere. Don't reinvent the wheel with research.

4.   Attend public meetings and collect information from other groups and government. Arrange meetings with decision makers to determine how they arrive at their policy positions.

MEMBERSHIP ENGAGEMENT

The most common form of public speaking for most campus organizing is the class talk. The class talk is an effective tool for communicating with a wide group of students and provides an opportunity to speak to all students regardless of their initial interest. For many, the class talk will be one of the only ways in which they hear about information from the campaign, especially if they are a working student, parent, or someone who is otherwise drawn away from campus any time outside of class time.

Delivering a Message

Public speaking is an acquired skill; it takes time to learn how to deliver a message effectively. Almost everyone gets better over time given consistent practice. Knowing the material meant to be delivered during public speaking rather than simply reading from cards or paper is the first step to being convincing and compelling. Being able to use personal comments and understanding the material to the point where it's second nature, where it's easy to identify the material with real life circumstances, will help the audience understand the message.

Practice

Practicing a speech or any other form of public speaking is the first step to ensuring that the emphasis is where the speaker wishes it to be. The audience will appreciate that the speaker has taken the time to craft a message that is easy to listen to. Fumbling through content or reading off papers will tell the audience that the speaker does not respect them or does not fully understand the content of the speech itself. Though it can be uncomfortable, no speaker should deliver a speech unless it has been practiced with trusted advisors beforehand.

Audience

Campus organizing requires public speaking in front of many different types of people. From first-year science students to PhD candidates in humanities, there is a wide array of perspectives. Knowing the audience and understanding what their initial response to the speech topic might be, but also the common notions in their group, will assist in connecting with that audience. Understanding that the audience is already generally in favour or opposed to the campaign can be a benefit. Examples, cultural references, and humor might change depending on the audience the campaign is addressing.

Confidence

A public speaker should be relaxed when they're delivering remarks. Along with knowing the material and practicing, speakers should develop a sense of ease with the content of the speech. Nothing about delivering the speech should give the speaker cause for concern.

Speaking slowly is critical to ensuring that everyone in the audience understands what is being said. Speakers have a tendency to speed up when they talk, particularly if they are nervous in front of the audience or if they feel a level of comfort with the content. For the most part, the audience will know far less about the content of the speech than the speaker. By speaking slowly, the speaker can ensure that the audience doesn't miss content because they don't already relate to what's being said.

Almost always, audiences will want the speaker to succeed. Even if a listener doesn't necessarily agree with the point of the campaign, they generally don't wish to sit through a speech that is nervously delivered by someone reading from a piece of paper. A confident speaker who is knowledgeable about the information can engage an audience at a higher level than someone who does not have a solid grasp of the information.

Successful Question and Answer Periods

A question and answer session can be a stressful time for a public speaker. Question and answer sessions have the effect of providing the audience a way to vocalize the points of the speech back to the presenters. Handling Q&A can be done in many ways. Answering people's questions should be a way of returning the conversation back to the main points of the speech. Just as in media relations, Q&A should never take the speaker away from the central point. It is always best to tell someone that organizers can get back to them and take their contact information. Given the nature of the situation, it may be best to have a volunteer or organizer ready to take down the contact information, and to tell the questioner that this person will be right with them to do so.

Follow Up

The best public speakers practice the material, understand the content, and express confidence to the audience. They also have a very strong follow-up plan to ensure that everyone in the audience is engaged in the next levels of the campaign. The first part of this is simply to collect people's contact information before, after, or during the speech. This will allow the presenter to follow up on questions that were asked during the presentation, or provide next steps for those who wish to volunteer in the campaign. Without a follow-up plan a speaker cannot know the success of their delivery.

TABLING

Information tabling is a critical tactic of almost every on-campus campaign. So long as there are hallways and common spaces on campus there will be information tables. As an organizer, the information table provides an opportunity for some of the most important forms of campaign outreach. The unique value of the face-to-face contact that tabling can provide to the campaign cannot be overstated.

Before setting up campaign tables, the collective should decide what the purpose of the table is. Is the campaign having hard conversations with opponents or simply spreading a message? Engaging in arguments may seem like a good idea, but they generally take away for the time spent informing those who would otherwise simply be in favor of the campaign goals. For example, campaigning for tuition fee elimination speaks to an issue broadly supported by students, and arguing with those who are against it means that organizers are focused on a very small minority on campus. In other circumstances, hard discussions will be the focus.

Organize for Success

The first step to successful tabling is to ensure that the table is organized. Those doing outreach should table with all of the necessary materials and with at least a brief rundown of the messaging, as well as practice delivering the message and an understanding of where there may be resistance from the audience. A neatly organized campaign table shows respect for those who are receiving the information. A campaign that has drink containers and food strewn across the table or where organizers are unapproachable will not be successful. Keeping organized and professional is the first critical step to successful tabling.

Timing

There's almost no bad time to set up a campaign table. Most campuses have students in attendance from early in the morning until late at night. Students who are on campus in the earliest hours of the day and the latest hours of the day will appreciate that organizers work to communicate with them, as they are often lost or forgotten about in campus engagement. Focusing on class change times and ensuring that lunch breaks are met with tables is the sign of an organized campaign.

Location

Location is important to the success of the campaign table. Setting up a table in a place most accessible to the traffic of students is best for communicating a message. Campaign tables that are unavoidable provide the highest opportunity for direct communication with students. The locations on campus that are best to receive the highest amount of foot traffic change during the day, from day-to-day, and along with the audience the organizers wish to reach. Placing organizers in front of the campaign table who are dressed appropriately, who seem approachable, who are smiling and friendly, will ensure that members do not feel uncomfortable when being asked to discuss the campaign.

Avoid Unnecessary Conflict

Any time people are confronted with information that challenges their view, there is potential for conflict. For the most part, students on campus will engage in campaign discussions with respectful interest. It is best to keep the message simple and present the campaign in a relatable way. Some will challenge campaigners to political argument or debate, and this should be avoided whenever possible. With the exception of those who are simply unsure about the campaign, most initial opponents will not be won over in the hallway on-campus. Conversion of those who disagree with the campaign is not usually the purpose of tabling. The purpose is to increase the reach of the message, engage potential volunteers, and ask listeners to take action.

Enthusiasm

Successful campaigners will build a relationship with every person who comes to the table. Someone who is friendly and happy to be talking about the campaign will inspire confidence. Someone who truly believes in the campaign will be happy to be tabling and talking about the issues. Using a friendly approach will ensure that those who wish to learn about the campaign feel comfortable, and those who wish to volunteer will be encouraged to come back.

SOCIAL MEDIA

Social media as an outreach tool is different than social media as a campaign tool. Using social media requires a message that connects with an audience in a way that makes sense with what they already know. Using social media as an outreach tool can sometimes mean using that outreach as a component of the greater campaign.

Social media can be a powerful tool. What social media cannot be is a replacement for face-to-face conversations and interactions. Social media cannot be the basis for developing an understanding among supporters of the greater issues involved in the campaign. If someone is interested in the campaign, they might use social media to find information that increases their understanding, but building majority support among students on campus requires dedicated education time, relationship building, and collective action. Success for the student movement requires a great deal of offline work.

A good organizer keeps up with technology, at least insofar as it will assist campaign work. This has become particularly important in the world of social media. Using social media tools that the base of the campaign is not connected with, or which the target of the campaign is not connected with, will cause them to be ineffective. Social media only works if the tools match the supporters and connect with the target in a way that can translate to effective engagement and campaign pressure.

In the same way that the collective will review and democratically decide upon strategies and tactics prior to engaging in them on the ground, the use of social media should undergo the same scrutiny. Social media strategies and tactics that don't support campaign goals will detract from them.

RELATIONSHIP BUILDING

There is a negative connotation to the term "lobbying," which is partially deserved. Lobbying in the sense of influencing politicians through direct means (with material goods or money) has no place in the student movement. However, the term is often conflated with building relationships, which is critical to campaigns of reform that characterize the student movement. Students' primary tool for influencing those who are the focus of campaigns is to make a robust case and mobilize popular support for a goal.

Establishing understanding and respect between students and supervisors, activists and administrators, people and politicians, is a skill that requires practice. A student reaching out on- and off-campus to decision-makers can engage in many approaches, including:

1. communicating with both decision-makers and their subordinates to inform the deliberations the campaign seeks to influence;

2.   offering to collaborate and lend organizational legitimacy to the work of the decision-making body;

3.   developing relationships with media and other groups that have a stake in the decision or the decision-making body;

Lobbying in this sense is about establishing a relationship with decision-makers to leverage their power to achieve a goal. Sometimes this will take a collaborative form, sometimes it will mean vocal and aggressive opposition – but it will never mean forgetting long-term goals for short-term gains. Revisiting the long-term strategy is important so that focus is not lost.

VISION AND OBJECTIVES

A successful lobbying plan should be part of a campaign strategy that sets out goals from the general to the specific. The specific, short-term objectives of the strategy serve to advance the campaign toward the greater goal. Any goal, if it doesn't ultimately lead to the success of the greater goal, should not be included in the plan. Principled policy reforms are rarely in-line with established government norms, and require organizers to develop and build support for new economic and political programs and arrangements.

Being able to express long-term vision is critical for relationship building. The student movement is not a source of social progress that exists in a world of reactionary despair. Some decision makers will actively wish to support greater access to education, but will not have the background and experience to do so effectively. Developing a supporter's understanding of long-term goals decreases the chance that ally's well-intentioned actions don't defeat the ultimate goal in favour of the short-term objective.

It is not difficult to point to examples of short-term solutions that work against the ultimate goals of the movement. Government may try to increase the number of available spaces for students to make education more accessible, but do so by increasing tuition fees. While more students may be able to get their foot in the door to a college or university, the broader impact is increased indebtedness of working people and a shift in enrollment toward those who have greater means.

NEGOTIATION

The most toxic elements of the campaign will show themselves when the time comes to build a relationship through lobbying. There is a cowardly tendency that prioritizes personal gain and individual relationships. This tendency amongst particular students' unionists will inevitably capitulate the long-term goals of a given campaign for the shallowest short-term victories.

Every lobby meeting should include an "ask" for the decision maker. For example, when meeting with the secretary to the University's Board of Governors about an upcoming vote on the institution's budget, the ask might be to include a presentation from the campaign to freeze tuition fees before the vote takes place. Asks will differ depending on how receptive the recipient is likely to be and if they are the ultimate decision maker.

Relationship building can be viewed as negotiation, in which there is a (generally unspoken) threat that the campaign will mobilize students to greater degrees until its goals are met. Respondents (those being lobbied) must either capitulate to the campaign or accept that they will face some measure of rebuke. For the most part, the only political power students have is numbers, so mass organizing is critical to supporting lobbying follow-through. If decision makers do not understand the threat to their power if they fail to yield, then the campaign cannot achieve its goal.

Functionally, there needs to be little difference between lobby meetings and other relationship building meetings. Just like meetings with coalition and solidarity allies, representatives should take detailed notes. Most meetings will require follow-up, especially if the person engaging in follow up was not at the meeting, making precise and accurate notes essential. It is also important to gather new information that might further the campaign.

Decision-makers who are on-side with the campaign require up-to-date information to support their advocacy for the cause. A well-run campaign will ensure that allies are kept informed at the right time. Whether decision-makers are convinced or not, it is best not to pursue meetings when there is no new information to offer and no new or growing pressure has been applied to support the campaign – it is a waste of time for both the campaign's representatives and the decision-makers and may decrease the priority given by decision-makers to further meetings.

Researching a decision-maker prior to a meeting can be a revealing process. Be sure that campaign representatives know what the person they are meeting with has said about relevant issues. A well-organized campaign will also prepare representatives with a decent idea of the public priorities of the decision maker in order to establish a rapport through focused small talk.

Remaining professional in the face of aggravation or when meeting with someone not worthy of respect is important. The campaign lives and dies on the battlefield of public opinion and student mobilization. The campaign does not depend on winning an argument with a decision maker who is being crass or has a particularly egregious policy position. Even a justified level of aggression is usually never going to lead to the best outcome for those depending on the campaign to succeed. Lobbying should be backed up with mobilization to be effective.

Decision makers will appreciate when meeting participants come prepared. Representatives should consult their notes when in doubt, and prepare written overviews or analysis of proposals to leave behind for them to read. Even if they don't review the material, the collective can at least say to students and the public that the decision maker was provided with the information and chose to ignore it.

After lobby meetings, be sure to send a message thanking the decision maker for meeting and following up on any outstanding questions. Write a report on the meeting and supply it to the campaign's organizers.

MEDIA OUTREACH

Mass publications, the complex of corporate, not-for-profit, and worker media institutions with public audience, are a key form of communication for campus organizing. Developing a media strategy is a basic part of campaign planning, even if the intention is not to engage with media outlets.

Not all publications, journalists, or editors are created equal – and each has its own role to play. Media outlets always have an angle, or a bias toward some particular set of political positions, and it is important to determine this before engaging with each.

Does the issue being addressed by the campaign have a noteworthy impact on the target audience of the media outlet? This is usually central to having reporters and editors pay attention to a media engagement strategy. In established media outlets editors will usually assign stories that cover social and economic change, follow a story for which there is already a "buzz", or are being advanced by someone with a relationship to the outlet.

Putting out a short statement or message with credible and newsworthy information is more effective than overloading reporters with unnecessary content. A press release should provide all the points that the campaign wishes to have reproduced by the outlet. Information should be presented as it is wished to be reproduced, and exclude all other information.

MESSAGE

The campaign message, sometimes referred to as a message box, is a set of points that representatives will seek to have repeated and validated in the media. Nothing but the points in the message box is important to the campaign. The message should deliver a clear perspective in a way that is compelling for the audience.

Any time a representative is preparing to engage in media work, a message should be established and collectively reviewed.

Building A Message Box

Usually a reporter will not only reach out to campaign representatives. Even though the campaign is the voice of truth, journalists will work to find opposing views to include in the story in an often-confused attempt at balance and fairness. It is important to appreciate and understand the opposing arguments, and especially the reasons that the audience finds them compelling. Understanding the motivations of the audience is critical to preparing a compelling message.

There are four questions that can help systematize the development of a message.

1. What will the campaign say about itself and the collective organizing it?

2. What do opponents say about the campaign and collective?

3. What does the campaign say about opponents?

4. What do opponents say about themselves?

There are several traps that are easy to fall prey to when crafting a message box. Academic terminology, overly complicated explanations, or otherwise incomprehensible intellectualism should be avoided.

A message box includes the critical points of information a campaign seeks to convey at the time of interview or publication. The collective should review the arguments for and against these points and decide upon the strongest. It is important to develop an understanding of the audience's expectations and assumptions. For example, a publication that speaks to the elderly will require the message to use terminology and reasoning that is digestible for older people.

Crafting a good message takes deliberation and conversation. Observing the following criteria will help:

> Be concise. If stated effectively, the facts will allow the audience to come to the correct conclusion.
>
> Be clear. The audience should understand what the campaign seeks and why. Do not be sarcastic.
>
> Be consistent. Be repetitive and avoid changing the message during the campaign. If done effectively, the story an audience reads in a newspaper will be the same as one from a campaign leaflet.
>
> Be compelling. Facts make for convincing arguments, as long as they are stated in a way that the audience cares about.
>
> Be conflictive. If the message doesn't conflict with commonplace assumptions or the opposition then there is no reason to share it. Contrasting values with the opposition can help the audience understand why they should come to support the campaign.

When crafting a message box, consider how the story will be told from person to person. No one approaches their friends and simply talks at them with facts. People tell stories that have an interesting narrative. It is essential to highlight the part of the story that is

newsworthy or, even if the campaign receives media calls, no one
will pay attention to the headline.

The audience will pay more attention to the message if it relates
directly to them. Keeping a story local, even if it relates to a matter
of government based in a far-off city, helps people see the connection
to them.

Stories about individuals are more attractive to most media outlets
than accounts of policy. Personal stories help the audience identify
with the issue and see how it affects regular people. Abstract
examples or academic theories are rarely compelling to those only
hearing about the story on the radio or television.

Staying On-Message

Maintaining the integrity of the message box is a skill learned
through practice and experience. It is commonplace for
inexperienced spokespeople to feel the need to answer every question
put to them. Answering every question will dilute the message and
put control of the dialogue in the hands of the reporter.

All responses to an interviewer should return the discussion to the
message box. If a question is asked that the spokesperson doesn't
have an answer for, it is always more advisable to say that they don't
know than to make up an answer. Innocently, in the pursuit of
compelling quotes, or through malice, reporters may ask questions
that seem difficult to relate to the message box. Unless a reporter is
being particularly aggressive, campaign representatives should be
able to steer the dialogue back to the message box. The following
phrases are examples of how to return to the message box:

> Here is how I see it…

> The heart of the matter is…

> The most important thing is…

> I'm going to emphasize that…

When you step back and look at it…

What we are talking about is…

Actually...

We're focused on…

At the end of the day…

Former-Prime Minister Stephen Harper displayed superb message discipline during his time at the head of Canadian government. When confronted with questions about the destructive and self-serving policy of his governments, Mr. Harper often asserted, "That is simply not true, …" and would proceed to reiterate message points.

While members of the collective will eventually be able to repeat the campaign's message in their sleep, it takes time and repetition to fully communicate the message to the audience. Few will follow every twist and turn in the politics of a campaign, and many will miss the message of the campaign if it is not reiterated time and again. In a world of political campaigns, corporate marketing, and other public discourse, a campaign requires widespread repetition to cut through to the audience, especially if the message challenges commonplace assumptions and norms.

Representatives should engage in mock interviews with other members of the collective as practice. This will allow for criticism and self-criticism about interview skills and the message box.

MEDIA RELEASES, ADVISORIES, AND STATEMENTS

A media release is a message to media outlets about the campaign with a suggestion about content to publish. The media release allows the collective to spread its message on its own time in its message box and makes it easier for reporters to create content.

Typically, media releases will contain the following:

> Headline: this is how the release captures the interest of editors and writers. The headline should be brief and catchy.

> Dateline: containing both the release date and the city or town in which it is released.

> First paragraph: briefly describes the who, what, when, where, and why of the story.

> Quotes and body: provide printable information to assist the writer. Quotes should invoke a strong argument and be supported by information in additional paragraphs.

> Boilerplate: a staple, infrequently changing portion of each release that gives the writer background on the collective.

> Contact information: phone numbers and other contact information for spokespeople assigned to the release.

> Backgrounder: usually included in media kits for complicated subjects, but not required or expected at all times. Backgrounders provide enough detail for reporters to ask more educated questions of all involved.

In addition to the typical media release format, statements and media advisories also serve distinct purposes in media relations. Statements are a one-way form of media communication that allow the collective to deliver its message while making it clear that no additional comment will be made at that time. Statements are used often, and can be shared on social media as a way to show support for a particular position.

Media advisories provide information about a particular upcoming event or action, allowing reporters to prepare to attend. Advisories provide all the information a reporter needs to get to a newsworthy event. If a media release is issued on the day of the event, it should be issued late enough in the day that reporters who attend in person have the first opportunity to cover the story.

REPORTERS AND OUTLETS

Campus organizers face challenges when it comes to any sort of relationship building. The duration of a campaign is often only one to two years, so it may be difficult for organizers to develop any sort of relationship with reporters. Making an effort to find media workers who are allies, or at least interested in covering the campaign truthfully, can be a benefit.

Reporters are under no obligation to help the campaign or the collective. Treating media workers with respect and professionalism can help develop the relationship. Phone calls and messages should be returned promptly – immediately if possible. Traditional media outlets will have reporting deadlines, so ask when that is and be sure to provide comments with enough time for deadlines to be met. Treating media workers with disrespect won't just damage the relationship with reporters, it will also cause the campaign lose coverage.

Maintain a contact list of media workers who have covered the collective's work. Be sure to take notes of the interest reporters display in their questioning, as it will illustrate their thinking and inform how the campaign approaches them in the future. Contacting reporters directly when there is an existing relationship helps both the campaign and the reporter.

For many, there is no such thing as "off the record." Be cautious.

LETTERS TO THE EDITOR

Many newspapers have pages dedicated to reader submission letters. Letters to the editor allow the campaign to deliver its message unfiltered and for free. While newspapers have lost circulation and following in recent years, letters to the editor remain one of the most read sections. Newspaper readership has remained strong among seniors, who tend to vote in stronger numbers than other demographics, so consider the audience when submitting letters.

Letters to the editor compete for the limited print space in a newspaper. Long letters will usually not get printed. Keeping the letter below 200 words is a commonplace and accepted standard. Whenever possible, it is best to relate the letter to a story that the newspaper is already covering.

OPPOSITE THE EDITORIAL PAGE (OP-EDS)

Opposite the editorial page pieces, commonly referred to as opinion editorials or op-eds, are longer form submissions to a newspaper than a letter to the editor. These articles, ranging from 300 to 1,000 words, feature the particular knowledge of an experienced individual who is not a reporter for the publication.

Like letters to the editor, op-eds allow the writer to deliver a message for free and without interference. Many publications print no more than one or two op-eds per issue, thus there are fewer opportunities for op-eds than letters. Campus newspapers are often starved for content and will likely welcome op-eds to fill space. Make sure to call editors to ensure there is print space and an appetite for the op-ed ahead of time.

In contrast to letters, op-eds can take some time to fill out an argument with supporting details. It is best to start the piece with a "punchy" or interesting statement and have the detail come after. Where letters are often too short, op-eds should include a call to action for the reader.

EVENT PLANNING

Planning successful events is a common part of effective campus organizing. Event planning takes into account many variables. Is it a commuter campus or are there residences? Are there many international students who will attend? Is the campus urban or rural?

Making events successful means ensuring first that they fulfill a purpose in the campaign strategy. Spending time on events, even interesting or well attended, is worthless unless it advances the campaign strategy.

Pulling off a successful event requires creating a plan that covers all aspects of the event and ensuring that each part can be carried out. The best event planners create contingency plans for hiccups on event days. It is particularly important to have backup plans when working with volunteers.

Having a diverse group provide input on large events will assist organizers in holding inclusive events. Effective mass organizing, building to events such as all-student assemblies, requires consultation and communication with and between groups and constituencies on campus. Many will be cautious about a campaign or organizing collective they are unfamiliar with, but will participate in events based on the motivation of people they trust.

Budget

Organizing an event starts with a budget. Outline expenses and make sure each can be covered. Most obvious might be food and equipment rentals, but there are many. Neglecting expenses can prove troubling as planning for events moves forward. Include contingency for unforeseen expenses.

Limiting the cost to participants is essential to organizing students to attend events. Financial barriers such as cover charges or long-distance travel costs will restrict participation.

Time and Location

Finding a good event location means taking several factors into account. When considering a space, work backward from the overall goal. For example, if the goal of the event is to draw one hundred students from a specific faculty to an organizing workshop, start with finding locations accessible to those students.

Be mindful of acoustics, wheelchair accessibility, parking, transit times, and other events taking place in the area. Use stage risers so that speakers can be seen, and ensure that a sound system is available if the event will include more than thirty people. Interpreters, working in sign or spoken language, often require at least two weeks to schedule time for an event, and are far more effective when provided written material before an event.

On-campus events are very frequently in conflict with other events and regularly scheduled courses. Some post-secondary institutions have a time set in the week, often between 11:00 AM and 1:00 PM, during which as few courses are scheduled as possible. This coveted time block is great for short events and information tabling. Contact the administrators responsible for space and bookings with as much lead time as possible to avoid a conflict with other groups on campus.

It is impossible to please or accommodate everyone. Some students will only be able to participate in events during evenings, and others only during break periods. If the campaign seeks to reach a mass audience of students, a mixture of times, locations, and accommodations will likely be required. Take into account institutional closures, religious days, public holidays, and exam timings. If an event is to have alcohol present, organizers should consider that many post-secondary students are under the legal drinking age or will wish to avoid alcohol, and making an accommodation may increase participation.

Communication

No one will come to an event they don't know about. Usually, fewer people will attend an event than the total number who commit beforehand. Organizing large open meetings requires robust communication and, depending on the content, active convincing.

Communicating about events can be so involved that there are full-time professions dedicated to it in the private and commercial world. What the collective will lack in professional and monetary resources, it must make up for in organizing face-to-face outreach. Social media and print materials can help raise awareness about events, but success will usually only come from direct communication between organizers or volunteers and potential participants.

The success of an event can be partly pre-determined by event communication. If work has been undertaken to make an event as inclusive of all students as possible, communicate this to potential attendees. Ensure that everyone promoting the event is clear on the message and purpose.

Timetable

A timetable is a chronological breakdown of each phase in an event. A precise itinerary of the event should be drafted in the planning process. The timetable will include pre-event and post-event timings to ensure that setup and clean-up are included. A fulsome timetable will help event planners assign tasks to participating organizers and volunteers.

Once a timetable has been drafted, the next step is to make a task list that includes each organizer and volunteer. Deadlines and clear communication will help set expectations. Volunteers want to be there and want to do a good job, so make expectations as clear as possible and let them be met. Micromanagement is often off-putting and can convey a lack of trust in the volunteer's capacity.

Pre-Event

The pre-event period begins as soon as planning for an event is underway. When drafting the timetable, it is best to focus on the work being done during the twenty-four hours prior to the event. This will include setting up rooms, welcoming guests such as invited speakers, preparing audio and video equipment, and seating participants.

It can be helpful to set aside a few minutes on the morning of an event to have a last-minute check in with organizers. Provide people enough time to note issues that have arisen.

During

During an event, there will be no time to make decisions in a group. Make certain that point people are assigned for areas of responsibility, and that a limited group or individual knows how each task is progressing. Well-organized events will have a note taker recording details and issues for evaluation afterward.

Afterward

Immediately after the event will likely be the time to tear down any temporary materials. If there are separate volunteer teams for setup and clean-up, hold a short meeting before the setup team leaves and the clean-up team starts. Volunteers cannot be thanked enough, so make sure to do so.

It can be helpful for collective decision making to write down reports about campaign events and actions. Include information about attendees, if the timetable was followed, and any hiccups in the process. Since students don't usually stay on campus for more than five years, or less in the case of colleges, it can be a benefit to have a written record of work done in the past.

Food

Few things attract students with no other investment in an event better than free food. While budgeting for food must be done carefully, it should be a priority provided there are available funds. Offering – and promoting the offering of – different types of free food options, such as halal, kosher, vegetable-based, and gluten-free food, may draw a greater number of participants.

Programming

Canada is a country of many nations struggling for recognition and self-determination. Acknowledging the territory of the nation or nations on which events take place should be included at the beginning.

Inclusive programming is important for social events. A campaign that makes particular effort to not only welcome all students, but also show respect for event attendees' communities, backgrounds, and struggles, will be better received. If participants in a campaign event feel excluded or alienated, it is a failure of the collective.

Information in presentations and speeches is not effective if it cannot be consumed and considered by all attendees. Asking speakers to avoid acronyms, jargon, and speaking too fast may be beneficial. Remember to consider sign and spoken language interpretation, as mentioned above.

Safety

Take safety seriously. For example, a students' union in British Columbia has in the past dropped pumpkins from great heights to have them smash on the ground, symbolizing a drop in tuition fees. This sort of event requires organizers to take many precautions to ensure that no one is injured. For events with speakers or presentations, be sure to announce any graphic or disturbing content beforehand. If there is the potential for medical emergency, ensure that someone with first aid training is present.

Evaluation

Once the group has everything written down take some time to re-evaluate the plans. Ensure that the plan meets the goals that have been established. The collective may wish to have a good balance of events that will attract as many people as possible. Make sure that there is enough time between events to ensure that they can be well organized, and that activists and volunteers don't burn out. After this, create an individual plan for each event that assigns tasks with a timeline for completion.

VOLUNTEER DEVELOPMENT

A small collective can engage in a small campaign, but to have a major impact a campaign needs to scale up. Working people usually do not have the resources to fund professional campaigners and professional organizers for a mass campaign. Volunteerism is critical to the success of mass movements, to the development of a campaign, and to scaling the work of a small collective. Regardless of the issue, there are likely those willing to give up some of their time, if not a significant portion of their time, for the success of the campaign.

Attracting and Directing Volunteers

Organizers need to provide a number of critical supports to volunteers for them to be successful and provide value to the campaign. The campaign should communicate to potential volunteers a sense of purpose and urgency for the work that they are doing. If the campaign is really seeking to make material change and win significant reform, then volunteers will often seek out the campaign because of this.

Once the purpose has been established, organizers need to recruit volunteers. This means collecting contact information, developing a relationship, assessing abilities, and assigning someone to be responsible for skill development.

The campaign needs to train volunteers to complete the tasks for which they are volunteering. Volunteers who are not provided enough information about the nature of their tasks, the reason for the work that they are doing, or the way their work contributes to the end goal, will experience burnout. Training will provide the campaign with more experienced volunteers and ensure that those volunteers improve on their work as a part of the campaign.

Organizers should develop a schedule for volunteer work in the same way that a manager schedules shifts for employees. If the campaign is inspiring, if volunteers feel as if the reform will have a material impact on their life that they wish to sincerely fight for, then they will engage in the work with as much or more sense of urgency than regular employees. Providing schedule times, ensuring that wherever possible there are supports as if they were employees of an organization, will ensure the volunteers feel that the structure exists for them to succeed.

Volunteers work for free. However, there are many things that organizations can do to show thanks to volunteers for the work that they do. Without volunteers, organizing would be ineffectual. Organizers can never thank volunteers too much for the work that they do. In some cases, it might be appropriate to provide a letter of reference to volunteers if the work might be reflected positively in a resume. This sort of thinking will keep volunteers coming back to campaigns.

Inspire Volunteers

Volunteers won't be attracted to a campaign unless the campaign is inspiring. A campaign that seeks a goal people can identify with will draw supporters in. Those who have not been involved in any form of political action, or have only engaged in some minor political work, will come to the campaign as volunteers with no set of expectations developed from other sorts of campaign work. Inspiration is critical to developing volunteers who will put in the hard work to realize difficult goals.

Volunteers appreciate organizers who work with them. When organizers do not engage in the same tasks as volunteers a divisive culture can set in.

Volunteer Development

Volunteer development has several phases. The first is basic recruitment, in which the recruit provides information about their experience and their previous work to organizers. The next is that organizers assess the needs of the campaign and the current abilities of the volunteer. Organizers train volunteers to ensure that they are capable of performing the tasks that the organization requires. The goal of this work is to train people to engage in the repeatable tasks that will lead to a measurable development in the campaign.

Part of development of volunteers, and of others who are involved in the campaign, is being truthful about what it will take to win the campaign. Being honest with volunteers about the time commitment required for the campaign to be successful will develop a healthy trust between organizers and volunteers. Trusting volunteers to know their own limits and to communicate those effectively is critical to the success of a volunteer effort.

Recruit the Right Volunteers

Recruiting the right volunteers can take time and be a trial and error process. Sometimes people will volunteer enthusiastically to assist with the campaign and then drop off for reasons that are valid, and sometimes because of laziness. The fact of the matter is that the organizers cannot get hung up on volunteers dropping off from the campaign. Recruiting volunteers takes time, effort, and experience.

A campaign should seek to recruit the right people to achieve success. Those who are inspired by the message of a campaign will be prepared to give time and energy to its success. Sometimes those with an immense amount of volunteer experience or experience working on political campaigns won't be the best recruits, particularly if the campaign is seeking a reform that other collectives or organizations would see as too high an aspiration.

Recruiting a diversity of volunteers will assist organizers in reaching pockets of the audience who might not be susceptible to the advances of other volunteers or organizers. Including a diverse group of volunteers will add to the skill base of the campaign. Each volunteer brings their existing connections to the campaign, so a diverse volunteer base will support relationships with additional communities. Some volunteers will speak additional languages, which can be particularly valuable in reducing the cost of translating materials, communicating face-to-face with those who are not fluent in English, or providing insight into ways in which the campaign is not effectively communicating with certain groups.

Assess and Train

If organizers value the input of volunteers, they will work to improve the volunteers' abilities. Volunteers who feel enriched from campaign experience will be more likely to continue than those who feel that they are simply repeating tasks. Successful organizers will establish measurable criteria for a campaign, measure the impact of the campaign over time, and assess if successes or failures can be attributed to a lack of development among volunteers and staff. By undertaking this assessment, organizers can ensure that robust training is taking place where it is required.

BUILDING SOLIDARITY

People are divided. There is little end to the ways in which people are divided, by race, religion, sexuality, class, and more. However, the list of *reasons* people are divided is much more limited. Dividing people is a tool of those with power to maintain their power, by keeping the focus on petty divisions rather than the disparities caused by actions of the powerful.

Division is countered by solidarity. Solidarity is unity in action. Only by building solidarity that cuts through the artificial divisions between people can a social movement harness the political power of the masses.

In any social movement, such as the student movement, organizers must work with those the movement seeks to represent. A campus organizer must know intuitively the concerns and perspectives that characterize students' experience. From this connection with students, organizers can work to build solidarity through the following:

a.   showing active concern for the satisfaction of the material and spiritual needs of students;

b.   raising awareness of the connection between day-to-day issues and society's greater failings;

c.   respecting the intelligence of students, including relying on their joint experience.

The first part of building solidarity is showing active concern for the material and spiritual needs of students. This concern is not passive, and producing leaflets about the crisis of student debt in Canada is simply not enough to enamor students to a campaign for lower tuition fees. Solidarity requires inclusive education, agitation, and organizing to show students that it is worth their time and aligns with their values. Students, like any other diverse social group, will distrust any organization that fails to respect and defend their material interests and right to spiritual practice as a private affair.

The second part of solidarity is raising awareness of the connection between day-to-day issues and society's greater failings. As an example, it is not enough to call for a reduction in the cost of textbooks; the connection must also be made between the parasitic relationships of corporate publishing houses with post-secondary institutions. By linking students' problems to bigger failures in society, organizers can develop a solidarity that doesn't dissipate once a small victory or reform has been won. If students understand the sway of corporate publishers on education because of a campaign for affordable textbooks, they will be far better prepared to engage in campaigns against private influence of public colleges and universities.

Finally, respecting the intelligence of students and learning from their experience builds solidarity in the student movement. A single activist can spread awareness of an issue, build a list of supporters, and ask them to take action to reach a particular goal, but this is neither sustainable nor effective on a large scale. Organizers bring together students for a common purpose and provide tools and support. Then, those involved may pass on their new skills to others.

If students don't understand how to build the movement, their participation is limited to whatever direction they are given until they lose interest.

Relying on students' experience is important. Students in a particular program will understand how to convey a campaign message to those in their program in a way that students of other programs may not understand. People are dynamic, they have connections in various communities, and building solidarity means understanding what connections students bring to the movement.

COLLECTIVES

The three aspects of building solidarity can be applied within a collective of student organizers.

Internal solidarity is about building a collective that can operate as an organizer for the masses. In this sense, an organizer is not simply an individual with the know-how and drive to bring people together, the organizer is the already organized group that understands these tools and has the connections to be effective. Within the collective there are several important tasks to ensure cohesion. The collective should be trained from the outset to see itself as a group working to a specific goal, rather than individuals coming together for their own purposes or self-advancement. The work of ensuring cohesion in the collective is called combating liberalism.

Liberalism stands for the constant supremacy of the individual over the collective. In common parlance, liberalism is sometimes conflated with various anti-oppressive attitudes. In the context of the student movement in Canada, liberalism stands for unprincipled collaboration with whoever will advance personal interests. The first step to identifying liberalism is recognizing some of the ways it manifests itself.

Within the collective, be it a student club or the board of directors of the students' union, liberalism means avoiding helping a colleague because it is awkward or uncomfortable to raise a concern. The opposite, of calling out individuals in a way that takes away from their ability to fix mistakes, in public rather than at a meeting of the collective, is also unhelpful. It is easy to avoid productive criticism if one's own work is not directly impacted, but in the long run this practice detracts from everyone. Collegial discussion is how collectives work out their internal problems.

Disregarding the decisions and directives of the collective is another form of liberalism. This is particularly destructive when one demands special consideration for personal input but fails to heed direction or work for the success of the group. It is impossible to organize a greater number of students for action if the collective cannot count on the constructive participation of its own members.

This is only a short description of the phenomenon. The first step to combating liberalism is to set expectations that have the confidence of the group. Regular reporting and check-ins will ensure that the collective understands what each member has contributed and be able to make corrections where there are deficiencies.

COALITIONS

Coalition building is critical to the success of the student movement. While the day-to-day connections between student organizations and the other social movements may wax and wane, there is a persistent connection that must be solidified. These coalitions are reciprocal and recognize the importance of students standing with their allies, as well as allies standing with students.

Coalitions can be based on many different things. The most effective coalitions between students and other groups are based on points of unity. This means that students, as they are organized, agree to goals, strategies, or tactics that will be mutually undertaken with another group. For the sake of success of the campaign, differences of opinion about matters not related to the points of unity are set aside, at least for the time being. In this way, groups that have wildly different opinions on matters that are not relevant to the campaign can come together to have a major impact.

In order for coalition work to be successful there are several conditions that must be met. The students involved in the campaign must understand how the work of the coalition fits in the objectives of the student movement. At the same time, other members of the coalition must understand both how their input positively impacts students, and how students positively impact their objectives. At their best, coalitions mutually inform and activate the power of groups that have shared interests, such as students and workers.

Students' Groups

Students already organize themselves into groups for various purposes. Sometimes this is actively fostered by the students' union, as in the case of clubs and course unions. Campus newspapers that are student-run are also student organizations, although they require a particular approach that respects their journalistic nature. Students' on-campus groups often have a strong connection with their participants that can be essential in activating them politically.

Some student groups will have an elected leadership or volunteers who play key roles. Identifying these individuals and making contact with them is the first step to building a coalition. Even having simple friendly conversations can provide an organizer with insight into the type of students who participate in that group. For their part, student groups who are approached in a friendly and collegial way by other student groups will often appreciate the acknowledgment.

It is important to treat even the smallest organized groups of students with the respect of any other organization. By making formal contact, amply explaining the work of the campaign or the collective, and making a sincere request to give a presentation to the group, organizers can do much to win respect. Students will appreciate an organizer who respects their work, even if they there are differences of opinion or background. Providing campus groups with sample motions of support or template letters can go a long way to helping them, particularly if the issue is outside of their usual work.

All coalition work is reciprocal. By publishing a list of groups that have agreed to support the campaign, or otherwise thanking those who have thrown their organizational backing behind the collective's work, a small measure of that reciprocity is fulfilled. The other impact of promoting the breadth of support for the campaign is that it builds momentum among those who might otherwise be skeptical.

Campus Workers

Depending on the size of the post-secondary institution there might be many types of workers on campus. Almost all post-secondary institutions have academic workers, faculty, and support staff workers. Most institutions also have workers who support secondary services on campus, such as cafeteria workers. Workers in secondary services may be members of the same union as support staff workers, or they may they may have their own union, or they may be unrepresented. Graduate students who engage in teaching, marking, research, or other academic work are also workers.

The student movement would make little headway if it did not have organizational connections with the organized movement of workers, particularly as they are represented on campus. Faculty and support staff unions are the first place students will find solidarity on campus. Only by building mutual understanding and solidarity between students and workers on campus will students have success in campaigns.

Faculty unions, support staff unions, and students' unions often form campus coalitions. These coalitions are at their best when based on points of unity that respect the autonomy of all three groups. These points of unity often include demanding lower tuition fees, respecting workers collective bargaining rights, and common plans to mobilize for better post-secondary education.

Community Groups

Building solidarity on campus is an important first step in any campaign of organized students. Many campaigns, particularly those that seek a political change at the municipal level or any level of government above the Board of Governors of the institution, require coalitions that are broader than just the groups on campus. Reaching out to community organizations and social movements requires organizers to develop an understanding of the goals and participants.

Solidarity is reciprocal, and to establish a relationship of solidarity and build a coalition one group must initiate that process.

When engaging in a campaign to bring members of provincial or federal parliament to a particular decision, it is almost always required that a campaign take on community dimension. Few decisions, including those taken in the ministry responsible for advanced education, are decisions solely in the interest of a particular part of the economy. The success of any such reform campaign is dependent on the breadth of its mass support. Building coalitions with community groups and social movements can bolster the public support for a campaign that community or campus organizing simply could never achieve. Even when campaigning for a policy change on campus, the power of community support should never be underestimated. Decision-makers at the local level, particularly those involved in the Boards of Governors at colleges or smaller universities, have often faced the sword of public backlash.

Members of the collective will likely have connections with groups in the community, or other social movements. Building on these connections, while it can seem as if there is little of substance in common, is important for the long-term development of a campaign. Any organization that brings together workers on some level is fulfilling a social, economic, or political requirement for those individuals.

A list of potential coalition partners should be easy to produce by reflecting on likely supporters. A list should first be drawn up of organizations the collective already has connections with. After this, finding other community organizations or social movement organizations with local chapters can lengthen the list. These can include organizations that represent a particular constituency, that advocate for a particular group, that campaign on a particular issue, or bring together working people on some basis of cooperation.

While it is important to consider the in-kind or financial contributions that the campaign will receive from coalition partners, the collective should also consider the support and reciprocity that it can contribute to coalition partners' efforts. Solidarity is reciprocal, and beginning the relationship from a place of giving is a far stronger position. An organization is far more likely to commit its resources to a relationship if it has already seen value from the dynamic between the two organizations.

ORGANIZED SOLIDARITY

Even if there is a long-standing relationship with a coalition partner, many people will not have an understanding about that history. Endorsing campaigns and actions of one another is a low commitment way to add an organization's social capital and recognition to a campaign.

Letters of Support and Formal Requests

Letters of support are written to offer a helping hand when a coalition partner faces an acute issue. Writing a letter of support can identify a group or organization to a potential coalition partner or strengthen an existing relationship. Letters should clearly identify the group, spokesperson, members, and type of support that is being offered.

Relating the coalition partner's issues to the sending party's own issues or members can help strengthen their position. If a letter of support is being sent directly to the coalition partner to simply state that the collective is in solidarity with their struggle, it is often best to provide a few examples of ways the organization is willing to help. If the letter of support is being sent to the coalition partner's opposition, then stating the reasons for supporting the partner is best. It is important when sending letters of support to the opposition that the text is drafted with the coalition partner's input and a copy of the letter is provided to them.

Letters of support should include a description of the central issue at hand, and describe how it relates to the collective. Linking the issue to other issues, particularly ones faced by the demographic of the collective, will strengthen the coalition partner's narrative.

There may come a time when it is critical for the campaign to reach out and ask for help from select coalition partners, or a broad range of potential supporters. To do so, the first step is often to produce a formal request of support. Request for support should make it as easy as possible for coalition partners to understand the issue, to respond to the request, and to support the ongoing campaign. These formal requests should be followed up by face-to-face or telephone conversations that describe the issue and the sensitivity.

A formal request for support in the form of a letter should include a description of the issue being faced by the collective, with an emphasis on the urgency of taking action. Supporting research and descriptions of the impact of the issue can assist coalition partners in rapidly responding to the request. Making specific requests for support, through participation in events and actions, or through the provision of resources, will also make it far easier for the coalition partner's organizers to understand what they are being asked to do. Providing example motions for consideration by democratic bodies such as union executives or not-for-profit boards makes it far easier for those groups. By providing examples of assistance that other coalition partners have provided, it shows that there is already support for the campaign. Inviting coalition partners to an organizing committee can entrench their commitment to the cause.

Coalition Building

Coalition building is a long-term reciprocal process through which those organizations or collectives that are focusing on specific issues can come together to support each other for the success of their common goals. In the long-term, building a vast united front of social movements, including students and workers, is essential to harnessing the people power necessary to counter the power of the corporate world in capitalist society. No other power exists to counter the concentration of wealth and influence.

Coalition building can be a daunting process. Student organizations have particular challenges when it comes to building coalitions, because students are only involved in their students' union or other student organizations for the short duration of their studies. Other groups do not face this challenge, for example environmentalist groups or labour unions, because individuals who participate in those groups can do so for decades. Despite this, it is very possible for student organizations to develop important, supportive, and productive relationships with other organizations.

The most basic level of organizing between coalition partners is the simple alliance. In this form of organizing, formal and informal relationships exist between the two organizations. On this basis, the organizations support each other when asked to do so or when it is obviously necessary. This is an important form of organizing that is likely the most common between student organizations and other groups.

As coalition building develops it becomes more complex. The politics of organizations often play a role in their relationships with other groups. Navigating the sensitivities of organizational politics and developing a platform of unity is an important skill to study. Several organizations working together for a single purpose, or for the purpose of maintaining reciprocity and solidarity, can solidify the relationship in the form of a coalition committee. Coalition committees exist between students' unions and the on-campus labor unions, between organizations in a province working for increased minimum wage, and other similar examples. Establishing a coalition committee can sometimes be as simple as putting the call out to potential participants. Finding common points to work together democratically can increase buy in from each participant.

Starting the work of building a coalition is very similar to the work described in making a formal request for support. Putting out a formal call, followed by face-to-face or telephone communication to discuss the initiative is the first step. After this, setting a meeting time and requesting participation from the broadest possible group. It is important that participants understand the expectations for their participation. Producing an agenda for the meeting, having a respectful and experienced chair for meetings, and seeking input from each participant, will help ensure that participants come back to the next meeting. Organizing meetings should be productive and not waste people's time. The result of each organizing meeting should be action on the part of participants toward the goal; if this doesn't happen then something needs to change in the meetings or outside of meetings.

Determining the future of society may require moving beyond simple alliances to common fronts. A common front can include workers of all sorts, students, indigenous peoples, and others across the whole of society, and unites them. This is a step in establishing the level of solidarity required to transform society or combat particularly aggressive opponents. Defeating resurgent waves of fascism and overthrowing climate change denial are examples of issues that may require implementation of the common front organizing principle. In 1923, anti-fascist leader Georgi Dimitrov stated "…*the most immediate interests* of the proletariat of all countries, the interests of its self-preservation and self-defense, of repulsing the rabid offensive of capital, of securing its bread, shelter and freedom, as well as its *major class interest* - its final liberation from the chains of capitalist exploitation, both *demand imperatively the immediate formation of a united front in the trade union and political struggle, on a national and international scale*." The current environmental crisis and the rise of ultra-nationalism around the world cannot go unaddressed. These matters require that students' unionists study coalition building and solidarity.

Points of Unity

Every organization has its political sensitivities. Expecting allies and coalition partners to understand all of these sensitivities, particularly in expansive coalitions, is often impossible. In order to work together toward a common goal, it can be helpful to set out clear and democratic points of unity.

For every coalition, points of unity will be different. Points of unity are all the basic requirements for the coalition partners to work together. If there are requirements that haven't been included, a coalition partner can't expect the others to respect that requirement. For this reason, it is critical that participants in the coalition be open and honest from the outset about their sensitivities.

As an example, a coalition committee between students' unions and labour organizations on campus might set in place the following points of unity:

> Tuition fees should be eliminated. All coalition partners' representatives on the Board of Governors will vote against tuition fee increases.

> Collective bargaining must be respected. Coalition partners will share information with their members about any collective bargaining, strike, or lock out. Coalition partners will not cross picket lines.

> Racism should be challenged. Each partner condemns racism in all its forms and the coalition will act to protect the safety of all on campus.

> The coalition respects each partner's autonomy. No coalition partner will interfere with the electoral process of any other.

> The coalition will be co-funded. Each coalition partner will contribute to the resources of the group.

STUDENTS' UNION ELECTIONS

Students' union elections are critical events for campus activists. As a vehicle for action, the students' union is only effective when those on the side of truth and justice hold the reigns and are prepared to harness them effectively. No other on-campus student group is likely to have nearly the same financial and human resources to engage in political activity. Thus, the fight for the orientation of these organizations is an ongoing struggle between various political schools, faculties, and social currents.

Generally, a successful electoral effort will follow the following steps:

1. slate building;

2. platform and message creation;

3. materials production and training;

4. robust member communication; and,

5. strict adherence to electoral officers' rules and dictates.

Why Run for Students' Union Office?

For the most part, students' unions across Canada have a section of their constitution that includes advocating for the elimination of tuition fees, or similar policy, such as universally accessible public post-secondary education. Running for students' union office is about building the student movement into a powerful force to achieve this goal. It takes commitment and skill to make advances along the path to better education.

The campaign itself is an opportunity to inform and educate members of the students' union (all students who attend the institution or a specific campus). This aspect of the campaign is particularly important if the campus is one of relatively little political action. It is also an opportunity to mobilize students and illustrate the effectiveness of political campaigns. This is a level of inspiration that can be delivered from a true student leader.

Members of the students' union generally want to know more about the students' union. While it may not be at the top of their mind, students understand that they pay a fee to the students' union and will expect some level of accountability for that money. There is nothing inherent in the relationship between a students' union and its membership that will make them think that the organization is anything but a service provider. It is the work of the students' union election campaign, and the work that is done afterward, that instills the understanding among members that the students' union is a political organization.

Getting Started

If a candidate wants to run in an election, now is the time to get started. An election campaign takes an immense amount of planning and organizing to be effective. It is never too early to begin to do the work that will make the election campaign successful. This includes building connections on campus by engaging in political fights that are incidental to the work of the election campaign and finding broad support.

There are several critical points in a checklist for a strong election campaign. Most important is having a candidate or group of candidates who can draw broad support, are effective campaigners, will be effective leaders once the election is over, and (in the case of a slate) who have a general agreement and points of unity. It's critical to have a base of supporters who believe in the candidates and their platform. Supporters need to not just believe in the platform points, but also to actively support them through helping the campaign. In addition to leadership candidates and supporters, campaigns need materials, money, and time. No one should be considered a candidate if they cannot commit the time to doing the work to win the election campaign and make their term in office a success.

THE SLATE

A slate is a group of candidates in an election with a common cause, platform, or organizing plan. Whether official or informal, building and running a well-organized slate can be an effective tool in winning students' union elections.

This task list will help a slate organizer develop a good list of candidates:

1. within the existing core group (sometimes only a very small group) identify skills, perspectives, and personal qualities needed to effectively pursue a set of political goals for the year;

2. communicate with potential candidates both the requirements determined by the group and the existing group's goals;

3. explore with potential candidates their understanding of responsibilities associated with being elected to a students' union board and respond to their questions and concerns;

4.   determine if potential candidates would be able and willing to serve; and,

5.   develop a slate that, if necessary, assigns each candidate a position to serve upon election.

    Note: steer clear of overcommitted candidates who will likely be unable to commit the time or other resources to the cause once the election campaign has begun, or once the election is concluded.

Much like other organizations, slates often require a motivated central group to ensure momentum in the campaign is maintained. As an organizer, it is important to be aware of the sensitivities and sensibilities of the candidates on the slate. Since the election process may be new and candidates have other commitments, organizers usually play to people's strengths and only provide as much direction as candidates are able to undertake.

Evaluating potential candidates is an involved process. Each person's availability, skill, and political understanding should be weighed. Potential candidates that display undue concern for themselves individually should be categorically avoided. This is a part of the constant importance of rooting out any elements of liberalism in the student movement. Building a robust, effective students' union is hard work that puts the interests of the membership above directors; but liberalism eschews debate, it represents unethical neutrality, and it does harm to students and their movement. Winning reforms means waging political battles, thus an ideology that avoids necessary conflict has no place in the movement.

The difference between a slate and a political party is generally one of spontaneity. That is to say a political party persists between elections, makes commentary on and engages in ongoing events, and represents a political tendency; whereas a slate exists to advance a particular platform during a single election after which it becomes dormant or dissolves. Students' union elections at large universities often allow for slates, though it is less common at smaller institutions and colleges. There are often many rules to follow in the running of a slate for an election, which must be meticulously reviewed or the slate risks disqualification. It's important that candidates who are part of a slate have the right skill and grit to beat opposing candidates, function as a collective insofar as it will serve them to be candidates and members of the board of directors, and share a common vision.

Building a slate requires paying attention to several different things. As a slate coordinator or campus leader there are several pieces of information that should be taken into account. Good candidates will bring with them a track record of working for students before the election. This can include working as a leader in a club, volunteering for the students' union in the past, or holding another elected position on campus.

When organizing a slate, it's important to pay attention to the diversity of the membership. Members of the students' union should see themselves reflected in the diversity of the slate. It's also important that the faculties of the institution be reflected in some part, so that there is a common point of connection between individuals on the board of directors at the students' union and the students facing issues in their programs.

It's important when running an election with a slate that a full list of candidates is organized. Running a partial list of candidates, particularly against an opposing slate with a full list, will be less appealing to voters. Students don't want to vote for a slate that they don't think can actually manage the board of directors effectively. While a slate may not be a collective with a single unitary vision for the students' union, it may be an alliance of political tendencies, it's important that there are points of unity that the slate agrees upon, such as campaigning against tuition fees. It's important from the outset of organizing for the election to set expectations about the management of the slate and the relationship of members of the board of directors after the election.

The Platform

A slate's platform for a students' union election should be one that students will want to vote for. That may seem so obvious as to be silly, but it is a legitimate point. Many slates run on platforms that focus far too much on longer-term policy shifts and the fundamental goals of the student movement, but without tangible next steps for the students' union to pursue many voters are turned off. Students' union boards of directors hold office for one year, so students rightfully want to know what their representatives are going to do with their membership dues in the coming twelve months.

Platform points should highlight reforms that are achievable and be more or less numerous depending on the level of engagement of members. Reducing tuition fees is a central part of the elimination of barriers to education for all working people. Without substantive platform points the campaign is a popularity contest, but commitments to campaign for tuition fee reductions and student grants are important to focus a contentious students' union election on legitimate progress.

In addition to common financial barriers, there are other limiting factors to education. In a general sense, the slate will commit to combating oppression as it manifests itself, but specific campaign promises should focus on acute issues. For example, "We're going to stop sexism" appears a laudable goal, but it is nebulous and unachievable in the scope of the election – members will take note and the opposition might use it to deride the idea of combating sexism. Alternatively, "We will seek funding for anti-sexual assault training" is achievable and more precise.

It can be tempting to spend an immense amount of time building a platform that speaks to all students on campus. This is a fairly common mistake. A campaign platform needs to have three aspects: it need be specific, achievable, and widely supportable. By focusing on what unites students, a campaign platform can usually be carved out of a handful of issues. Slates through which candidates focus on what is different among students often end up with campaign platforms that are a long list of generally unachievable goals. The vast majority of students on campus are working class, meaning they come from backgrounds where they can't afford the high tuition fees of Canada, and they are united by the call to reduce tuition fees. Goals are specific. For example, narrowing down from "making education more accessible" to "reduce tuition fees by two percent" better communicates the slate's direction to members. Goals are achievable if the campaign can make a reasonable argument to voters that they can be reached within the time frame of the term. Voters will consider supporting goals if they are desirable and are presented with a viable plan to be achieved.

Materials and Training

Materials are an important aspect of a campaign. Most campuses have areas in each building where posters can be placed. It's important that the face of the candidates is laid out against a small amount of text that includes campaign points and the website's URL. If the campaign also includes some measure of call to action it's important that that be included.

Posters and flyers that are crowded with too much text will not be read. Producing a flyer or other print material with a list of candidates on a slate can help voters know who they need to vote for when they go into the ballot box, especially if the name of the slate is not listed along with candidates' names on the ballot. It's exceptionally important that a website be created, as many students, particularly on a large campus, will seek out information about candidates on the website.

A website need not be a complicated or expensive affair. The best websites provide insight to what has been happening within the students' union over the previous year, and provide suggestions on how to move forward concretely. Websites can include a list of endorsements with quotes, platform points, a sign up for contact information, and candidates' biographical information. It's best to avoid a website that has text essays about political or other issues, and avoid spaces where readers can comment. It may seem democratic to have comments on a website, but it simply provides a place for opponents to flood in with negative comments.

Campaigning

Election campaigning can take various forms. Many candidates will produce materials, engage in social media campaigning, and participate in students' union run candidates' debates. The most important part of campaigning on the vast majority of campuses in Canada is the face-to-face conversation. Students need to see that their representatives listen to them and have a clear platform. The face-to-face conversation is one of the most awkward skills to learn, but will serve the candidates after the election during their political campaign work. Simply approaching a student and saying, "mind if I talk to you for a moment?" will often provide an organizer a few minutes to converse about issues that they face on campus as well as the platform for the election and asking for their support. Asking questions of potential voters is particularly important; students want to know that candidates care what they have to say. An old adage says that humans have two ears and one mouth for a reason and they should be used in that ratio. This anecdote applies for candidates on the campaign trail. Face-to-face campaigning also allows candidates to build a list by asking for contact information from students.

There are some campaign tactics and strategies that will serve a slate or an individual candidate well. Seeking endorsements from well-known or popular campus personalities can go a long way to building trust among a broader range of folks than can be reached through face-to-face conversations. For example, acquiring an endorsement from leaders of clubs, and asking those leaders to promote their endorsement by emailing their own list or communicating it to their members, can go an exceptionally long way in communicating the campaign message to individuals that campaigners might never encounter on campus.

Communications

In addition to face-to-face conversation, there are a few different ways to communicate with members effectively. After collecting contact information through information tabling, approaching students on campus, or through other means, it's important to follow up using that information. Try not to flood followers with email, but be sure to provide them with information that is fresh and interesting about the election and about when to vote. Communicating when to vote and reiterating whom to vote for is a central part of communicating during an election. If a campaign has collected cell phone information be sure to have candidates from the slate sit down for a time and text every member of the list about when the vote is happening and reiterating whom to vote for. Social media platforms can allow peer-to-peer contact that is far more effective in ensuring that students go to vote. For example, having a friend tell another friend to vote for a slate is far more effective than meeting an individual in the hallway, so engaging students to do so is particularly effective. Following up with new contacts promptly increases the chance of maintaining their support.

ELECTORAL RULES

When slates break the rules, they get disqualified. This is particularly true if a slate is not organized by the existing establishment of the students' union, which may have installed an electoral officer favourable to maintaining a particular group or political trend. Strict adherence to the electoral rules, including seeking out descriptive assessments of allowable tactics from the electoral office beforehand, can be a benefit to the campaign. This does not mean the campaign will benefit from a moralistic adherence to campaign rules, particularly oppressive rules that infringe on the democratic process, simply that it is most often a strategic decision.

Nominations

In almost every election, candidates will be asked to seek nominations from fellow students on campus. Often, candidates will reach the bare minimum of nominations and submit the paperwork, a common mistake. On some small campuses this can be as few as ten students. On a campus of 10,000 students in which the minimum number of signatures is 100, candidates do themselves a disservice if they if they collect fewer than 1,000 nomination signatures on their paperwork. The reason for this is simple; by approaching students and seeking their nomination candidates achieve two important goals. The first is that someone who has nominated a candidate for

an election is much more likely to vote for that candidate in the
actual election than someone who has only heard about the
campaign afterward. The second is that the nomination period
usually begins long before the campaign period. By seeking a large
number of nominations, candidates are able to deliver their message
on a mass basis before their opponents are doing so, or at least
before the campaign period.

Protecting the Vote

Students' union elections follow particular rules. These rules are
spelled out in different places that include the relevant provincial
legislation regarding societies, the constitution and by-laws of the
organization, and potentially other regulations. It's important to
protect the vote from undemocratic activity, especially if there have
been accusations of election fraud in the past. Reviewing the rules
should be the very first activity in organizing election campaign and
the rules should be referred to often during the process. Anything
that would detract from the secrecy of the ballot should be
challenged with the electoral officer.

On some campuses, incumbent candidates and long-time staff might
seek to disqualify those they see as having a particularly different
agenda from the status-quo operation of the students' union. It is
important to communicate with the electoral officer about any
potential for disqualification and be clear and communicative to
avoid it. In every election students should have the opportunity to
appoint a scrutineer to watch the production and counting of ballots,
and every candidate should take advantage of the opportunity to
have a scrutineer.

ELECTION PLANNING

Planning for elections need not be that complicated. The first step is
to find out the number of votes that were cast in the previous
students' union election, and compare that to the total number of
members of the students' union. This will generally give an idea of
the number of votes that will be required to be in a candidates favor
for the election campaign to be a success. Once the campaign has

determined, in a general sense, the number of votes required to win the election, the campaign can work backward from that number to determine the required number of supporters in each faculty, among clubs, social groups, and on different campuses. It's also important to determine the limits on financial expenses during a campaign period according to the students' unions rules, and ensure that the campaign will be able to raise that much money.

It can be helpful to determine the number of required supporters in each physical building on campus. By breaking this number out, buildings can be assigned to volunteers and supporters to campaign in those buildings specifically. Assigning responsibility for building connections with students who attend classes in a particular building can be a more manageable way to campaign.

Common Mistakes

Quite often, potential candidates make the mistake of campaigning openly prior to the campaign being announced or the election being called. In most cases it would be a violation of the election rules to campaign openly to students about the students' union election before the election campaign period. Additionally, many candidates don't have the network, the supporters, or the understanding to build a full slate of candidates to run in the election – running a single candidate against a full slate is a surefire way to lose the election. While it can be an appealing prospect to be a students' union leader, this is not usually first thing someone should do when they first become a student. Connections are important.

One of the most common mistakes in students' union elections is the mistake of not campaigning. Most candidates have never run an election in the past, and have neither an understanding of the work required to win the campaign nor be effective afterward. Some candidates will simply be too cocky or uncomfortable with the process.

Contacting Members

Good candidates understand the membership of the students' union and believe in making their lives better. Asking members for their contact information is essential to deliver the message of the campaign and mobilize voters. It's important to get a phone number and email address for each person that is contacted during a campaign. If a student won't give a candidate their phone number or email address, then they're likely not going to vote for that candidate. Getting contact information allows candidates to follow up with that individual about the things that were discussed, but more importantly it allows for follow up to make sure that they get out and vote.

POST-ELECTION

Generally, once an election has been won there is a period between the end of the election and the beginning of the new term. During this "lame duck" time, the defeated outgoing leadership may act in their own interest rather than the interest of the students' union's members. It's important that an incoming board of directors continue to meet before their term starts, and that they review activity in the students' union office.

Lame duck members of the board of directors may seek to destroy records that implicate them in unethical activities, or incur vast expenses before their term ends. Incoming members of the board of directors should attend every board of directors meeting prior to when their term begins, and seek to have meetings or shadow sessions with outgoing members of the board of directors. Once the term begins, the newly elected board of directors is responsible for managing the students' union in the interest of the full membership of students. Any new director that does not engage in robust training for themselves, seek out experienced students' unionists for assistance, and otherwise prepare for the position is doing a disservice to their members.

STUDENTS' UNION DEMOCRACY

Holding effective meetings is the first organizational part of advancing a program for increased action, political participation, and student power.

The importance of holding meetings effectively, with appropriate use of time, and accomplishing the goals of the meeting, cannot be overstated. The board of directors is the brain to the students' union's body. The discussions of the board of directors represent the thinking of that brain. In any living organism, if there is conflict and an inability to determine a way to move forward within the brain, the organism could not be expected to function effectively. Similarly, if a students' union board of directors cannot determine a course of action, or determine of course of action in an effective way, then the organization cannot expect to succeed.

RULES AND REGULATIONS

Each students' union has democratic rules included in the constitution, bylaws, and policies that govern meetings of the organization. As is likely spelled out in policy, students' unions usually adhere to Robert's Rules of Order. Robert's Rules of Order are a long-standing set of meeting rules used across North America to govern meetings. Additionally, students' unions will be governed by legislation that dictates how meetings may be run, such as additional restrictions on quorum and notice.

While it is not important for each member of the board of directors, and certainly not each member of the students' union, to have a full understanding of every rule and regulation regarding meetings, the board of directors should receive sufficient training. The chairperson, staff, and others who assist in managing meetings should have strong working knowledge of the Rules of Order and other regulations regarding meetings.

Bylaws and Policies

The democratic rules set up by members and the board of directors are the most politically important to adhere to. This is not to say that it's unimportant to adhere to the law or the Rules of Order, but those are set out by outside groups and organizations. The constitution, bylaws, and policies of the students' union are the democratic will of the members of the organization. It is likely that the use of Robert's Rules of Order is spelled out in a bylaw or policy of the organization.

The students' union may have policies concerning a number of aspects of meetings. These can include time limits for debate, gender-alternating speakers' lists, and other specific rules. In addition to these, it may be possible for members of an assembly, for example a general meeting or meeting of the board of directors, to set up additional rules at the outset of a meeting. In many places around the world, particularly where there are no standard sets of rules, rules are generally adopted at the beginning of the meeting alongside the agenda.

While it may not be a formal policy, the students' union may have traditions and practices that have become entrenched in the culture of meetings. These are not enshrined and can be changed by the leadership of the organization, but it may take a concerted effort to do so. Greatly changing the flow and function of meetings, particularly when participants have certain expectations, can cause consternation.

Legislation

The legislation governing societies in each province may mandate restrictions and regulations for meetings. It is legally important that these are followed.

Rules of Order

As mentioned above, Robert's Rules of Order is a common set of rules used in organizations across North America. The rules generally reflect procedure used in meetings for legislative bodies. The rules are common because they are widely available and fairly easy to understand.

Using Robert's Rules of Order has several benefits for students' unions. The Rules of Order are intentionally organized to properly balance the rights of those on the majority of a particular issue with those in the minority. Generally, the rules protect from the majority having undo sway on the minority, and allow the minority to be protected from the majority while not being able to dictate to the majority. The rules also have stipulations that are meant to protect the dignity of participants and foster respect.

In addition to these benefits, the students' union is also provided an "out-of-the-box" system for efficient meetings by using the Rules of Order. Meetings are where the minds of an organization come together to synthesize a plan that is greater than the plans of each participant, which can only take place if meetings are organized efficiently and effectively.

PREPARATION

If plans are not made prior to a meeting, the meeting will most likely
be a failure. Planning and preparing for meetings is the basis for their
success, with failure to do so being the most common reason why
meetings are reported to drag on or fail to meet quorum.
Preparation includes drafting the agenda, reviewing the agenda,
discussing ideas with others, connecting with directors or members of
the assembly prior to the meeting – basically ensuring that
everything necessary for the meeting is arranged beforehand.

Planning for a meeting should include political and logistical
concerns, as both are related and necessary for success. The first step
in the political planning of the meeting should be to determine what
the goals and objectives of the meeting are going to be. From these
goals, the structure of the meeting can take shape. This includes the
order of business, the way that business is proposed, and the
preparation undertaken to provide participants enough information.
Generally, once a brief conversation has taken place about the goal
of the meeting, it falls to an individual to prepare a draft of the
agenda, based on which more discussions can occur about the
meeting.

Logistical planning is critical for the success of a meeting. For
example, if participants cannot arrive at the meeting because they
don't have information about the location, or do not have
transportation, then the meeting cannot possibly be a success.
Logistical questions include location, timing, and document
preparation.

Ensuring that the location and the information in the meeting are
accessible to participants is important. The only way to ensure that
the accessibility needs are being met is to consult with each
participant on a regular basis. The Rules of Order provide for
accessibility needs of meeting participants, but the rules cannot
dictate what happens outside of the meeting; therefore, it falls to the
leadership of the organization to be proactive.

Once the political goals for the meeting have been determined, and planning for logistics is underway, the organizer must communicate directly with participants about the meeting. This informal process will lead to far more success in achieving the meeting's goals. Allowing fellow participants time to think and question things that they know will arise at the meeting will prevent meetings from becoming derailed by confusion.

LEADING A MEETING

Every meeting has leaders. The best meetings occur when the chair of the meeting is well organized, competent, and experienced, and when the participants view their role as participatory leadership. A culture of participation should be fostered within the students' union in which each member understands they have a responsibility to provide input and support others in providing input.

Chair

Each meeting will have a facilitator generally referred to as the chair of the meeting. It is the role of the chair to ensure that the meeting flows smoothly, follows the rules, and adheres to the agenda. A strong chair will engage the meeting in a way that fosters discussion without imposing undue limits or restrictions on participants.

The chair should ensure that participants have what they need to contribute to the meeting. This includes assisting participants in making recommendations and submitting motions to the meeting. Even if the chair is personally opposed to the objectives of participants, it is up to the assembly to determine a course of action for the group, and the chair must have faith in the will of the assembly. Fairness and the consistent application of the rules will ensure that the nature of chairing does not become controversial in and of itself.

There are many types of personalities among meeting participants. Some participants will want to speak on every matter, and some will avoid speaking at all costs. An effective chair fosters discussion from all participants when it makes sense to do so. There may be, from time to time, participants in meetings whose intention is to disrupt the meeting or aggressively oppose a particular position. Managing contentious issues by fairly applying the rules and taking a moment to describe issues or highlight matters that are affecting the normal flow of business are signs of good chairing.

Participants

While the chair of the meeting is working to ensure that the process is effective and efficient, it falls to leading participants to ensure that the meeting achieves its political goals. Participants should engage in the same preparation and post-meeting reflection that any leading organizer does, even if not a part of the organizing team for the meeting. By viewing their role as a form of leadership, participants can consciously reflect on their contributions.

Meeting participants should arrive on time and prepared. Reviewing the agenda prior to the meeting, and ensuring that all of the material to support an argument is on hand are important steps to advancing a political position. Other aspects of preparation include ensuring that allies will be at the meeting and ensuring that they have a way to get there.

Leading participants in a meeting will speak only at the most opportune times to advance their political position and the meeting itself. When it comes to run-of-the-mill functional aspects of the meeting, such as adopting regular motions of process, leading participants will actively move and second motions to ensure that they are resolved in a timely fashion. By restricting the number of times that they speak, not dominating the speakers' list, and choosing their battles, leading participants ensure that the meeting can move forward steadily.

POST-MEETING

A common failure among organizers is to finish a meeting and then put their feet up with a sense of accomplishment. There are several post-meeting tasks that, if done regularly and directly after meetings, can increase the productivity of the students' union greatly. If meetings are intentionally organized to inspire and enthuse participants, then it is wasteful not to use that enthusiasm to ensure that the work discussed in the meeting takes place.

The first step in post-meeting organizing is to determine if the goal of the meeting was achieved, and ensure that next steps are followed through. If the goal of the meeting was not achieved there needs to be determination about why that is the case and what the next steps need to be to ensure that that goal is fulfilled in the next meeting or at another appropriate time. If the goal was achieved, the organizer must proceed with the appropriate follow through.

As far as the flow and logistics of the meeting is concerned, it is helpful to take notes during and afterward. If it is immediately important, these issues should be addressed right after the meeting. If issues are identified that should be resolved or dealt with prior to the next meeting, then the note should be taken to address it at the appropriate time. For example, if there were not enough chairs in the meeting space then that is something that should be addressed prior to the next meeting. It can be helpful to ask for feedback from meeting participants from time to time, but is not always necessary.

After the meeting, organizers will send communications to each participant about the work that they have agreed to do in the meeting. This can include task lists, minutes of the meeting, and other documents that show each participant's responsibilities. This allows participants to see the work that was discussed in the meeting moving to on-the-ground organizing, and for participants to hold each other accountable to the work that they agreed to do. It can be helpful for organizers to communicate directly with meeting participants after the meeting about their work, offering assistance and help where it's needed.

STUDENTS' UNIONS AND THE LAW

Students' unions, campus-based public interest research groups, and (sometimes) student newspapers are legally incorporated societies. As legal entities, they are ascribed legal requirements to follow, and by doing so can ensure that membership dues are collected, society status is maintained, and the affairs of the organization can be conducted with some manner of legal protection. The legislation covering students' unions is different in each province, and there is separate legislation covering those organizations incorporated at the federal level.

Law that outlines the legal rights, and requirements to retain those rights, of students' unions is called "right to organize" legislation. At many points in the history of the student movement in Canada, post-secondary institutions and governments have tried to challenge students' ability to organize. Right to organize legislation has most successfully been won in Quebec and British Columbia, with some progress made elsewhere, though students' unions exist in each province.

The students' union is two separate things at the same time. In one hand, the students' union is a legally incorporated society, and in the other hand it is the democratic will of students. From time to time, achieving the goals of the student movement requires students' union leadership to operate outside of the legal framework of the students' union. For example, engaging in civil disobedience is by its nature counter to the law, but has been an important part of student struggles for justice in Canada and around the world. Understanding the law, and what work of the students' union falls outside of it, is important to making informed decisions.

The British Columbia Example

British Columbia is one of the only provinces with legislation mandating post-secondary institutions to collect and remit membership dues to students' unions. This legislation is the result of political activity on the part of students advocating for the right to organize.

Prior to 1994, the collection and remittance of students' union membership dues was entirely at the discretion of each post-secondary institution's Board of Governors.

In 1994, the Canadian Federation of Students-British Columbia successfully advocated for the right to have membership dues collected and remitted. This legislative change was the result of a yearlong consultative process undertaken by the BC Government. Along with remaining in good standing with the Society Act, the preparation of audited financial statements by students' unions, including their provision to the post-secondary institution, was required under this legislation. An institution's Board of Governors could cease collecting students' unions membership dues if, in the Board's opinion, the students' union was improperly managing its finances.

In 1999, after over a year of concentrated lobbying, again on the part of the Canadian Federation of Students-British Columbia, both the University Act and the College and Institute Act were further amended. These amendments require that students' union membership dues be approved by referendum, and explicitly set out that students may choose to be members of provincial or national student organizations. The acts now required students' unions to provide annual correspondence to colleges and universities setting out the amount of membership dues to be collected in the following academic year, noting the provision of audited financial statements to members, and assurance that the students' union remains in good standing with the registrar of societies.

SOCIETY GOVERNANCE

Students' unions are governed by legislation and by the democratic decisions of the organization. The external legislation generally provides some measure of protection for the organization, particularly when it comes to the collection of membership dues from students. The internal documents of the organization, such as the constitution and by-laws, are long-standing expressions of the democratic will of students. It's the responsibility of the board of directors of the students' union to ensure that the democratic will of students is executed according to the constitution and bylaws that they set out.

The legislation governing students' unions has several common requirements, regardless of province. Students' unions are generally required to hold annual general meetings at which they present audited financial statements to the membership. Even where not required, some students' unions engage in this practice as a matter of transparency. Where it is required, students' unions must report to the applicable registrar of societies (or corporations) that an annual general meeting was held and any changes to the bylaws or the composition of the board of directors.

Constitution

A students' union constitution, generally not longer than a single sheet of paper, describes the reasons for the organization's existence. Commonly this list of reasons for calling the organization into existence includes fighting for universally accessible public post-secondary education, providing services to students, and providing students an avenue to participate in democracy. Often constitutions will also include the official name of the organization and a clause regarding the windup of the organization.

Bylaws

Bylaws are a detailed description of the structures of the students' union. Many students' unions will outline, in a broad sense, the positions on the board of directors in the bylaws. Bylaws also describe what the requirement is to be a member of the organization, and how to alter membership in the organization. Bylaws generally outline the processes of democracy within the organization. This includes the process for referenda, general meetings, and the administration of proxy votes for all meetings. It is not uncommon for bylaws to prescribe a set of rules, such as a Robert's Rules of Order, for use at all board of directors and general meetings.

Policy

Where bylaws fall short of describing each process undertaken at the students' union, policy steps in. The students' union's policy on processes within the organization often describes everything from how students interact with the health plan of the organization to how political campaigns are considered prior to adoption.

General Meetings

General meetings are the highest decision-making body of a society, with the exception of referenda of the whole membership. Generally, students' unions are required to present audited financial statements to their membership at general meetings. Quite often, general meetings are also the place for a report of the students' union's board of directors to membership about the work undertaken in the previous year. Depending on the bylaws of the organization students or directors may be able to submit motions for consideration. Just like meetings of the board of directors, general meetings can only deal with certain business if quorum is met, meaning that enough students participate in the meeting for the decisions made there to be recognized.

On certain occasions, the students' union leadership may call a general assembly that is not necessarily a general meeting of the organization. General meetings are a specific type of meeting, with the power to amend bylaws and adopt certain policies, whereas general assemblies are simply open meetings of the whole membership of the students' union. The reason that a general assembly might be called rather than a general meeting would be to inform students about the closure of campus because of a strike, to organize members about a particular political issue, or another such purpose. The requirement for notice and the standard for quorum do not exist for a general assembly in the same way that they do for general meetings.

Member Responsibilities

The legislation regulating legal societies usually creates the following division of membership:

a.   Members. Usually, members are ascribed rights with no responsibility, although some students' unions set responsibilities for members. General members have the right to run for and elect directors and to change the constitution and bylaws.

b.   Directors. Directors have the right to manage the society and the responsibility to uphold legal duties to the organization.

c.   Officers. Officers implement the day-to-day work of the society. They may be elected directors of the organization.

Each group is usually described in the constitution and bylaws of a students' union.

LEGAL DUTY TO THE ORGANIZATION

Both directors and officers have obligations to their societies. These obligations are set out in legislation relating to not-for-profit societies (e.g. the BC Societies Act), tort law, and the internal documents of the society. Society officials have responsibilities to act reasonably and with care in the interest of the organization they serve, as well as other responsibilities determined by their membership.

Constitution, Bylaws, and Policy

As the constitution of the society outlines its basic purposes for existence, it most likely does not outline specifics of directors' responsibilities. However, if, individually or collectively, directors are not pursuing the goals set out in the constitution, members may remove them from office.

Bylaws usually cover specific responsibilities of directors. Many societies' bylaws will include descriptions of the responsibilities of each position, as well as for the board of directors as a whole. Additionally, the society will have bylaws that restrict how money is spent that directly limits directors and officers. The bylaws may contain penalties for directors who fail to uphold their responsibilities.

The society may also have policy that outlines how directors are expected to carry out the duties described in the bylaws.

Fiduciary Duties

In law, a fiduciary relationship exists when any person is in a position of confidence and power over another, including when a person is in such a position in a society. The person in power, the "fiduciary", is responsible to act in the best interest of the other person or society. In order to uphold this responsibility, the fiduciary must neither make personal profit from their position nor allow personal interest to conflict with their duty.

Directors have a fiduciary relationship with their students' union. Thus, they must make decisions in the best interest of the society and have a number of additional duties. Students' union directors have a duty of care, duty of loyalty, and responsibility to avoid conflict of interest.

Duty of Care

Directors are responsible to handle the affairs of their students' union with the skill and due diligence of a reasonably prudent person. A reasonably prudent person is defined in law. Directors are required to make informed decisions, meaning they can be penalized for decisions made without reviewing all of the relevant information. This also means the directors are required to execute their duties such as attending meetings, obtaining expert opinion when it's necessary, and ensuring that the records of the society are kept properly and filed with government at the appropriate times.

Directors are granted authority in their position on the board. Failing to act in the interests of the society when it is necessary is a breach of fiduciary duty. This means that, if by failing to act they do damage to the organization, directors are then in breach of their duty. The opposite is also true, and directors who exceed the authority or ability to act that has been democratically granted to them are also in breach of their fiduciary duty. This includes actions that are outside the scope of the mandate of the students' union.

As a part of the duty of care, directors are required to follow applicable laws, including the students' union's internal documents. Duty of care also requires directors to ensure that decisions of the students' union, including decisions made by members through referenda and general meetings, are being implemented. If there comes a time where the law and the democratic will of students conflict, directors are forced to make a political decision about how to move forward.

Standard of Care

The standard of care for students' union directors legally requires exercising the discretion of a reasonably prudent person. Directors as a group or as individuals who fail to uphold their fiduciary duty may have personal liability. As such, directors are required to exercise the standard of care.

In determining if a director is liable for some harm or damage to the students' union, a test is undertaken about that person's actions. The director's actions are evaluated to see if they are those of a reasonably prudent person under the same circumstances. This is generally the legal benchmark to determine processing liability. Individuals who are being assessed as reasonably prudent people have their level of experience, understanding and ability taken into account during this process, meaning that someone who has an accounting degree may be held at a higher standard of reasonably prudent person in the case of embezzlement or misuse of students' union money.

There are several issues that may cause individual directors of the society to be personally liable to repay damages. These instances are said to "pierce the veil" of not-for-profit society liability. Examples of these issues include failure to pay employee wages, failure to make regular payments to government, violation of environmental standards or health and safety standards, or violations of other laws. Breaches of fiduciary duty as a director may bring the director liability. Various events, subsidiaries, and businesses of students' unions can increase the potential liability for directors.

Not-for-profit society liability insurance exists to limit the potential cost for societies and individual directors when certain problems arise. For many students' unions, maintaining liability insurance is required under their bylaws or because of agreements with the institution. By and large, liability insurance does not cover acts of individual directors, or groups of directors, who engage in deliberate libel or when they are acting in bad faith.

Duty of Loyalty and Conflict of Interest

The duty of loyalty requires that the work of directors be carried out in the interest of the students' union. This duty is meant to specifically limit self-dealing and conflict of interest. Self-dealing is when a fiduciary ensures that the business of the students' union provides them a particular and unique benefit. Student directors must avoid action that would be in their own interest or the interest of other individuals or organizations above the interest of the students' union and its membership. This is a critical fiduciary duty.

Legislation regarding not-for-profit societies (e.g. the BC Societies Act) dictates that directors disclose at any time if they may be in a conflict of interest.

Conflict of interest exists when a person in a position of power stands to receive undue benefit from their involvement. A director may be in a conflict of interest, as an example, if they seek to have the students' union procure resources from a particular business with which they have a connection. Endorsing contracts with friends or family is a conflict of interest.

MEMBERSHIP DUES

As previously described, students' right to organize legislation is different in each province. As a director of a students' union, it is absolutely critical to understand the current rules and regulations that govern students' unions. In order to protect the students' union from losing membership dues, or in a broader sense from students' unions losing ground in the right to organize legislation, it is important to ensure that existing rules and regulations are followed.

Each year, the students' union should communicate with the administration of the institution about membership dues collection for the coming year. Depending on the legislation of the province, or agreement between the students' union and the post-secondary institution, there may be a process spelled out for communicating about membership dues collection. For greatest transparency, and to ensure the moral high ground in political negotiation with post-secondary institutions, it is important that the audited financial statements be completed and presented to the membership each year.

As a not-for-profit society, a students' union is required to file documents with the registrar of societies and or companies each year. These filings can include a regular annual report, a change of directors report, or a report of special resolution. Anytime there is an election, a general meeting, or members vote to change the bylaws by referendum, a report likely needs to be filed with the provincial government. Often these can be found on the Internet and filed with a nominal fee. Ensuring that this work is done, alongside providing all the essentials of financial statements to students, gives those agencies and the institutions little ground to revoke students' union membership dues.

LEGISLATION

Societies

Provincial, and in some cases federal, legislation governs the activities of not-for-profit societies. Under these rules, societies are required to elect a board of directors, adopt bylaws, hold annual general meetings, and file reports with government. The rules generally set out minimum numbers of participants (quorum) in meetings for them to be considered valid to conduct most business, as well as other stipulations about democracy within the society.

Post-Secondary Institutions

All public colleges and universities are brought into existence through legislation, be it an act respecting all post-secondary institutions of a particular type, or legislation respecting an individual post-secondary institution. This legislation determines how post-secondary institutions are governed and if students are afforded any elected positions on those bodies. In some cases, there are explicit regulations on students' unions in this legislation.

Privacy

Students' unions deal with members' personal information in many forms. If the students' union runs a health and dental benefits plan, it will usually have access to a significant amount of personal and legally protected information. Provincial governments and the Government of Canada have legislation governing the use of personal information.

Human Rights

Human rights law sets out to eliminate inequality and discrimination based on specific criteria. These laws also provide for those impacted by discrimination based on the prescribed criteria to seek amends. Generally, human rights legislation prohibits discrimination on the basis of race, colour, gender, ancestry, place of origin, religion, marital status, family status, physical or mental disability, sex, sexual orientation, or age.

Alcohol

Events and activities in which alcohol is involved are regulated by provincial legislation. This legislation places the responsibility of protecting attendees on the event holder, and generally requires the purchase of licenses.

STAFF

Working with staff means dealing with the number of variable factors that can change how the relationship develops. While it can seem as if staff relations are an exceptionally "business-y" aspect of students' union work, it is one of the reasons that the student board of directors was elected. Students expect their elected representatives to manage the students' union, including staff, in their interests.

Employees

There are generally two forms of employment legislation – one respecting non-unionized employees and another respecting members of a union. Regulation respecting non-union employees includes minimum wage, duration of workdays, statutory holidays, and other matters. The students' union's relationship with unionized employees is governed by a collective agreement between the employees and the employer, which is adjudicated by a court known as a labour board.

Staff Relations Officer

The differences between staff relations from students' union to students' union are too variable to describe in this volume. It is best, if not required, to assign a specific director or officer to be the staff relations officer. This member of the board of directors should be the sole person responsible for dealing with staff issues and reporting back to the board of directors. By having an individual, or a very small committee, responsible for managing staff, the board of directors limits both liability and confusion.

Legal Assistance

At any point during staff relations matters, a board of directors of a not-for-profit society may seek legal assistance. Students' union boards of directors may seek legal assistance to deal with matters relating to unionized employees and collective bargaining, or to deal with matters of individual employees through contract negotiations. Seeking legal assistance is absolutely in the purview of the students' union board of directors, and they need not have approval of staff of the students' union to do so. If, given the matter at hand, the question among directors is whether or not legal advice would help to avoid liability, the correct answer is usually to seek legal advice.

STUDENTS' UNION FINANCES

Across Canada, students' unions are financed by membership dues that are collected when students pay tuition fees to their post-secondary institution. These dues are usually set by referendum of the entire membership of the students' union, and are reflective of the political decision of students to collectively finance organizing. The leadership of the students' union is in a position of privilege and responsibility to dispense with these resources in the interest of achieving the organization's goals. In order to maintain membership confidence in the students' union, as well as prevent control of the organization by unethical and self-interested individuals, it is critical to maintain high standards of transparency and accountability.

Membership Dues

Membership dues include all of the universal mandatory fees paid to the students' union when members begin their program, semester, or other portion of their studies. Membership dues do not include health and dental plan fees, as not all students necessarily pay for health and dental coverage, and some may opt out of the program if they're covered elsewhere. Both universal mandatory fees, and health and dental benefits plan fees, should be set by referendum of all members of the students' union. These are the resources allocated by students to their political organization for the purpose of achieving the goals spelled out in the students' union's constitution.

Membership dues are set by referenda where all members are eligible to vote on the initial rate, and in most cases the rate of annual adjustment. Referenda also determine whether or not there will be any particular additional fees. For example, a students' union may run a referendum for a $1 fee meant to be allocated to clubs and other student activities, and then in subsequent years run referenda to increase that fee, decrease the fee, or eliminate it. In many cases, student-run papers or radio stations are funded through specific fees or general media fees that were set by referenda.

Finances are Political

Students' union finance is political. The membership dues allocated to the students' union by the democratic vote of members is a political investiture in the goals of the organization. It falls on the shoulders of the students' union leadership, year-over-year, to uphold the responsibilities of spending these resources in the interest of achieving those goals. One of the most common failures of students' union leadership is the failure to connect the resources provided by members to the goals of the organization.

Over the years there have been several times when local, provincial, and pan-Canadian student organizations failed to achieve their goals or to reach a position in which they could strive toward their goals because of the of lack of resources. It is important that students' unions are allocated enough resources by members to realistically engage in campaigns for education reform. Building a student organization to the point of adequate resources requires several things. The organization must be credible and responsible with the funds it is provided to inspire confidence in members to increase funding to the organization. Additionally, the funds that are provided to the organization must be allocated to its goals.

Credibility and Reputation

The political efforts of the students' union will be immeasurably hampered if it does not have credibility and a strong reputation. The organization must be able to achieve its goals, and act credibly in the eyes of members, in order for them participate meaningfully in its work. This is a dialectical process where members who view their students' union despairingly will refuse to participate in its activities, thus reducing the effectiveness of the organization. The reverse is also true, where members who view their students' union favorably, and believe that the leadership of the students' union is acting in their best interest, will be more inclined to participate in its actions and, thus, the organization will be more successful. It is important for these reasons that students' unions avoid financial mismanagement, as it will impact the organization's reputation.

Outside of the organization, the reputation of the students' union is integral to all of its relationships. Students' unions that fail to produce basic financial documents, present their finances to members, or engage in sketchy financial transactions will be shunned from other political organizations. Coalition partners in solidarity shouldn't be put in the position of having to work with an organization that has a reputation for poor financial accountability.

FINANCIAL DOCUMENTS

There are several standard financial documents that are required by students' union leadership to undertake their work in making reasonable and realistic decisions about the allocation of resources, as well as reporting to members about finances. These documents include the students' union budget, monthly or quarterly statements of total spending, the audited financial statements, bank statements, and cheque requisition forms. The first step to ensuring that the students' union is transparent and being accountable to members about the resources it requires is ensuring that each of these documents is prepared in due course.

Budget

For students' unions, the budget is not simply a mechanical document that allocates resources to this or that function of the organization. The students' union budget is a political document that represents the priorities of the organization for the coming year. The first step to building a budget is reflecting on the actual revenue and expenditures of the previous year, which can be found in the organization's financial documents including the audit. The leadership of the students' union takes the information from the previous year; makes estimations about revenue and expenditures for the coming year, and sets out priorities for the use of resources. While some students' unions put their budget to a vote of members at a general meeting, it is more common to simply have the board of directors adopt the document.

Revenue and Expenditure Reports

The leadership of the students' union should receive monthly or quarterly reports on the year-to-date revenue and expenditures of the organization. This information is critical to ensure that the organization is on track to collect the estimated revenue for the year, that the money budgeted for particular items is being spent properly, and to determine if adjustments need to be made to spending for the rest of the financial year. These reports will generally be produced by the organization's bookkeeper, which may be a staff member or an individual or external organization contracted by the students' union.

Audited Financial Statements

Audited financial statements are a set of financial documents compiled by a third-party accounting firm. In provinces where students' unions' right to organize legislation is more developed, there are requirements about the reporting of financial standing. For example, in British Columbia, legislation requires each students' union to prepare financial statements and present them to members at an annual general meeting, as well as communicating that this is taking place in order for the institution to collect and remit membership dues. Financial statements will include a breakdown of how membership dues were spent over the course of the previous fiscal year, may include a breakdown of wages and benefits for both staff and members of the board of directors, and include notes about large expenditures or nuanced aspects of the organization's finances.

A third-party auditor compiles the financial statements of the organization. It's the responsibility of the leadership of the students' union to liaise with the auditor to ensure that the information is presented in a way that makes sense to members and reflects the reality of the financial position. Over the years, if the students' union retains the same auditor, that firm will develop an understanding of the workings of the organization and be able to better assist in presenting financial information.

Statements and Expenditure Records

Each month, the students' union receives a statement from its bank or credit union outlining all of the activity on its account for the month. The signing officers (described below) should review bank statements each month to ensure that the activity on the accounts reflects the revenue and expenditures expected by the leadership. If there is any activity on the organization's accounts that seems suspicious, signing officers should review it against expenditure and deposit records, and take steps to ensure that no further activity can take place until the matter is resolved.

All revenue received by the students' union will be deposited in the organization's accounts. When this takes place, there is a record of the deposit that will be kept in the organization's offices. When expenditures take place, by cheque or credit card, then there will be documentation to reflect this. All expenses will go through a process to ensure that they are reflective of the will of the organization. These include the filing of a cheque requisition, which is signed off on by two signing officers for the organization, then the creation of a cheque, which is also signed by two signing officers. Between these two documents, as many as four people will review expenditures before a cheque is released.

FINANCIAL ACCOUNTABILITY

The elected leadership of the students' union, the board of directors, is responsible for the financial direction of the organization. Depending on the size of the students' union, the delegated authority for the production of financial documents might be complicated or confusing. To breakdown the confusion it makes sense to clarify the ultimate responsibilities for each of the tasks related to finances.

Elected Leadership

The overall financial responsibilities of the elected leadership in the students' union include the establishment of a budget for the organization, oversight of revenue and expenditures, regulation of financial controls, and establishment of policies related to finance. The policy or bylaws of a particular students' union might delegate the responsibility for drafting the budget to a particular member of the executive committee or a staff person. There may also be policy in place that puts further stipulations on financial interactions of the organization, including the limits on the amount that may be spent with a resolution of the board of directors.

When engaging in a budgeting process, the leadership of the students' union must be prepared to set priorities for the organization for the year ahead. Once the draft has been produced it falls to the group to review the documents, make suggestions about the budget, and move forward together. Depending on the size of the students' union, there may be programs in place such as clubs and course unions that the organization has a history of funding or a responsibility to fund. Making determinations about the funding meant for subordinate organizations can be particularly controversial. In these decisions, and other decisions made about funding campaigns and services, it may be beneficial to the organization to engage in consultation with members. Consultation may be as simple as inviting members to present to the board of directors, or a more involved process, depending on the level of membership engagement.

In order to ensure that membership dues are collected at the correct rate the students' union must communicate with the post-secondary institution about these for the coming year. In British Columbia, students' unions are explicitly responsible for providing a letter to the institution that outlines the fees to be collected in the upcoming year, any referendum held to establish or increase fees, and that a membership meeting has taken place during the year in which audited financial statements were presented to members. In any province, it makes sense to the students' union to issue annual communication with explicit criteria about the remittance of membership dues to the institution.

Signing Officers

The students' union will likely have a policy that outlines how signing officers are appointed. Signing officers are those who have been specifically delegated the authority to sign off on financial expenditures and contracts for the organization. Signing officers are responsible for ensuring that all contracts and expenditures are allocated correctly within the budget, that they follow the will of the board of directors, and that they are executed properly.

The financial accounts of the students' union, be they with a bank or a credit union, will require signing officers. New signing officers are generally chosen upon the commencement of a new term of office for directors. Often, the financial institution will require meeting documents, such as minutes, or other material in order to appoint new signing officers. Depending on the policy of the financial institution, new signing officers and old signing officers may be asked to participate in the in-person meeting.

Staff

Generally, there are staff people responsible for aspects of the financial operation of the organization. While the responsibilities for financial oversight rest with those who hold a fiduciary duty, usually the board of directors, there may be responsibilities placed on the shoulders of staff according to their contract or collective agreement. It is the responsibility of the board of directors to ensure that staff people have adequate training, knowledge, and experienced to uphold their responsibilities.

The leadership of the students' union should have a strong understanding of which staff people have been delegated which responsibilities. If it is the case that there is no member of the board of directors specifically responsible for reporting on financial activity, this may fall to a staff person. Asking financially responsible staff to prepare reports on a monthly or quarterly basis is a reasonable request for the board of directors to make in order to ensure transparency.

Members

At the organization's annual general meeting, the board of directors will present audited financial statements for members to review. While this is only a legal responsibility in some jurisdictions, it is a minimum standard for financial transparency. Members should reasonably expect that the organization that represents them would be able to provide an audited report of its revenue and expenditures for the previous year.

In many cases, the students' union will have a bylaw or policy regarding the review of financial documents by members. In some jurisdictions members will have a legal right to review financial documents or receive a copy of the documents for minimal cost. It may be a benefit to the organization to establish a practice in which any member who seeks to review the financial documents is provided time to do so with a member of the board of directors or a knowledgeable staff person who can explain details and answer any questions that they might have.

STUDENT GRIEVANCES

Most students' unions in Canada provide a service to help students with academic and non-academic appeal. Students' grievances come in many forms. Matters of individual importance require a skillful approach that respects the student's privacy, adequately follows institutional policy and law, and protects the students' union. Individual advocacy may include, or evolve into, lobbying, campaigning, or other public action. Much of this depends on the response of the institution to the grievance of the student and if the official or formal process isn't already in place.

Students who seek assistance from the students' union with a grievance may not understand the applicable policy or regulations regarding the matter. Sometimes matters to do with an instructor's behavior will appear to the student to be a simple academic matter, when there is much more at play. It's the responsibility of the students' union to determine how best to approach the matter and assist the student in dealing with the formal regulation and policy. This may include assistance in appealing a specific grade, addressing inter-personal problems with an instructor or professor, and defending the student against allegations and penalties. From time to time, these matters require the students' union to assist in dealing with harassment.

There are some students' unions that assign the work of assisting students with grievances to an elected student. Most often, student advocates are staff of the students' union who have an understanding of the institution's policy and some background in casework. Regardless of the advocate's position, they are responsible for maintaining the privacy of students, assisting them to the best of their ability, and ensuring that the students' union does not overstep or fail to assist a student.

Working with the post-secondary institution, students' unions should seek student grievance policy that is easy to understand and manage, has clear and fair procedure, and ensures that all institutional policy is upheld. The more that students and post-secondary institutions work together to ensure that students feel policy is robust and fair, the less time and resources will be required to be spent on student appeals. This collaboration is in the interests of students, the institution, and the public.

Student Rights

Students have a number of legal rights at post-secondary institutions in Canada. These rights are expressed at the highest level in the Canadian Charter of Rights and Freedoms, and at lower levels from provincial charters of rights and freedoms and policy of the post-secondary institution. Students also have the right to evaluation and assessment that is fair, as well as fairness in all of their interactions with their instructors, professors, and administrators.

In the regular course of study, students have the right to equal access to resources on campus. Within a class, students have the right to equal access to materials for study. Students who feel that they have had unequal access, or face discrimination, have the right to proceed through formal measures to address their issues. These measures are almost always outlined in the post-secondary institution's policy.

When engaging with the appeal policy, students also have the right
to expect fairness and due process.

Students who are accused of any form of misconduct have a number
of rights. These rights include the right to due process under the
institution's policy, the right to be heard and defend themselves in
the quasi-judicial process of the institution, and the right to
impartiality in the adjudication of their appeal. As a part of ensuring
that the process is fair, students have the right to access documents
that relate to their case, including records of proceedings, of minutes
of oversight committees, and test marks. Students also have the right
to appeal to higher bodies within the institution. Any restrictions
placed on these rights by an institution should be challenged by the
students' union.

Student Responsibilities

While it may not be entirely clear to students, and there might not be
enough work done to make it clear, students have the responsibility
to understand the policies and procedures of their institution. Just as
in a higher-level court, ignorance of the applicable policy and
procedures is rarely accepted as an excuse. Ignorance of institutional
policy is not grounds to dismiss an accusation against a student, or
basis for a student to appeal decision. The exception is when it can
be materially proven that the institution failed to communicate that
information to students. Institutions often include comments about
students' responsibilities in the syllabus of the course, making it
difficult to make an assertion that there was a failure to communicate
the information.

Students are responsible, under the policy of the post-secondary
institution and legislation or the law, to act in a way that is
reasonable and suitable in the education environment. If a student
disrupts the learning environment, it's the responsibility of the post-
secondary institution to limit that disruption or remove that person
from a place where they can disrupt others. Students should expect
to complete assignments on time, and maintain academic integrity,
and avoid plagiarism at all times. When students fail to maintain

high personal academic standards while attending a post-secondary institution, it can be difficult to represent them as a student advocate.

Faculty Responsibilities

Faculty behavior can be a basis for student complaints and appeals. Faculty members are responsible for being knowledgeable about their course material and related subject matter. If faculty fail to be prepared for class, fail to show up to regularly scheduled classes on an ongoing basis, or the material they provide to students is not appropriate to the course, this can be a basis for student appeal. In a general sense, faculty are responsible for following the syllabus that they provide students at the beginning of the course, and ensuring that the syllabus is sufficient to meet the criteria of the program as set out by the senate or education council of the institution. Changes to the syllabus, changes to grading criteria, or other changes to the course that are not revealed to students with advance notice, and without student approval, are often a basis for student appeals.

Individual Advocacy

The students' union may be required to help individual students with many types of concerns, academic and non-academic. By helping deal with concerns through informal and official channels, the students' union plays a key role in representing students and helping them deal with matters of great personal concern. These matters may relate to any individual, structure, or policy within the institution, including instructors or administrators. The students' union's advocate acts solely on behalf of the student or group of students to make sure that they are treated fairly.

A skilled advocate will listen carefully to the grievance of the student and help that individual determine what the broader nature or understanding of their concern is. Gently questioning a student about their concerns ensures that a simple academic appeal does not have deeper dimensions, such as discrimination. Advocates assess the situation for each student specifically, provide information on what avenues are available for the student to seek assistance, and help them understand and follow through with the process described in those policies.

Depending on the student's relative ability to represent themselves and follow through with the institution's procedure, the advocate may take a more active role. The role of the advocate is usually determined through consultation with the student. The advocate will weigh the particularities of the case, especially the likely individuals involved, given that casework can be disruptive to the delicate relationships and personalities within the institution. The advocate may make inquiries, file paperwork, or explain a student's position, but should always do so only when there is explicit approval from the student.

At all times, advocates should maintain the confidentiality of records relating to the case. All actions of the advocate should be recorded for use within the case and so that there is a strong record documenting the steps taken to defend students.

The goal of the advocate when dealing with an individual student is to help them understand the process, manage their own participation in the process, and help them resolve their issue. Through all of this the advocate should ensure that the student is treated fairly within the institution's policy. Cases of individual advocacy for post-secondary students are student-driven and advocate supported.

Confidentiality

Maintaining confidentiality is an absolutely critical part of individual advocacy. The only time that a student's information should be divulged by an advocate is when the student has given consent for the sharing of their information. An advocate should only divulge information where appropriate and in the interests of the student to individuals and bodies of the institution that are part of the appeal process, and never in an informal setting. When a student's future hangs in the balance based on an appeal process, the students' union can have an immense individual impact on that student's life.

ACADEMIC GRIEVANCES

An academic grievance is any problem the student has that relates specifically to coursework and grades, and excludes issues of discrimination, harassment, or other interpersonal issues.

An academic grievance may be based on:

- student evaluations;

- unreasonable expectations from faculty; and,

- issues of fairness.

Students are usually expected to communicate with their instructor or other appropriate individuals about informally resolving the matter. After this first step, there are often other avenues for students to seek satisfaction. These include appeal processes and formal complaints.

A student may face an academic issue that is not specifically related to a faculty member. These appeals relate to other, often more administrative, aspects of the post-secondary institution. These issues can include problems with tuition and administrative fee assessments, registration and course concerns, financial aid issues, errors on transcripts, and complaints about the management of programs outside of the classroom.

Post-secondary institutions place an immense importance on proper academic conduct for several reasons. For example, medical programs relate academic honesty and integrity with students' ability to engage in healthcare practice. Overall, a post-secondary institution relies on its ability to recruit students, and failure to uphold high standards of academic honesty and integrity could be harmful to its reputation. Students appreciate an institution that holds high standards of professionalism, integrity, and honesty, because the institution's reputation reflects well on them as degree holders after the completion of their studies.

Academic misconduct is activity that violates established principles or policies within a program, department, or institution. Usually, academic misconduct relates to activity engaged in by a student or researcher that would furnish them with undue benefit or reduce benefits to others. Academic misconduct might be any case in which academic material, such as documents, assignments, data, or research, is presented as one's own work even though it has been stolen, falsified, altered, or otherwise misattributed.

Particular focus is paid to a form of academic misconduct called plagiarism. Plagiarism occurs when one person presents the work of another as their own, which is widely considered theft in the academic community. Direct or paraphrased quotes without attribution, or the purchase of content that is submitted as one's own, are considered plagiarism.

There are many potential ramifications for being deemed guilty of plagiarism, or other academic misconduct. These ramifications include the loss of marks or grades, especially regarding particular assignments for which there is an accusation of plagiarism. If there is an ongoing concern about plagiarism and a student is found guilty, the ramifications can include failing a course, removal from the program, or suspension or expulsion. The ramification for a student is usually set out in the policy of the institution; it is likely that a letter will be added to the student's record.

INSTITUTIONAL ISSUES

Students will seek assistance from the students' union for issues that are not related to their academic standing, or may be related to, but do not stem from, their coursework. This includes the treatment they receive from their instructors when not related to coursework, policies and procedures at the post-secondary institution, or if they face harassment.

At every point in which the student interacts with their institution there is an opportunity for the relationship between the two to break down. Be it in the financial aid office, the counseling department, speaking to an instructor, or elsewhere on campus, these interactions can take on a negative dimension. Most frequently, students will seek assistance in dealing with matters of unfair, unethical, or harassing behavior following points of interaction. However, students may also face issues of violations of institutional policy, including matters of privacy.

WINNING APPEALS

The role of the advocate is to help students win appeals. While some will argue that the students' union should play a role of ensuring fairness, this leaves students to themselves to win the appeal. Only fighting for members can achieve the maximum success of student appeals and build confidence in the students' union.

Requests for Assistance

The first step to any appeal process is that the student involved contacts the students' union. At the point of contact it is important that the students' union collect basic information from the student. Often times students will go from office to office seeking assistance for their issue, only one of which is the students' union office, and by not collecting contact information the students' union may forfeit the opportunity to assist a student.

Listening to a student about their issue is a critical part of creating an effective appeal. Listening is not a passive interaction; the advocate must inquire about specifics where they think they may be relevant to the case. The more information that is gathered, the better the advocate will be prepared to assist the student in their appeal process. Collecting dates, including a detailed timeline of events, is often critical to the success of an appeal based on ongoing behaviors. Taking very detailed notes is important, as is not leaving the notes where other people might come across them. Member privacy should always be taken seriously.

A successful advocate will discuss the matter with the student in a way that clarifies all potential grounds for an appeal. Often an student will be entirely unaware of the potential grounds for an appeal, so it falls to the advocate to develop arguments in support of the their position and clarify that position for them. Students will generally not know all the policy of the post-secondary institution that they attend, and the advocate should attempt to assist them in winning their appeal without burdening them with the minutiae of the appeal process, except when necessary. Typically, the grounds for appeal are spelled out in the policy of the institution. These can include failure to follow policy on the part of an instructor, or other institutional employee, or issues of discrimination that violate policy or provincial and federal law.

Once the advocate has gone over the matter with the student, and the two have worked together to create a written timeline of events, it's up to the student if they wish to move forward. If the student wishes to proceed with the appeal with the assistance of the advocate, it is then time to file. Close attention must be paid by the advocate to the type of matter being appealed so that the appeal is filed under the correct policy of the post-secondary institution.

Filing Appeal Paperwork

While this is not always the case, most institutions will have some appeal format or form written into or included with the policy. It is important that appeal paperwork include the evidence required to support the argument for the appeal, but not the argument itself. Usually, appeal paperwork will not require complete justification for the appeal, as this is left to the student or the advocate to deliver verbally. In some cases it will be required in writing during filing, in which case it should be provided.

If possible, the appeal should be broad, rather than specific, so that there is a greater array of grounds on which to make arguments. As the appeal proceeds through face-to-face meetings, to the hearings, and potentially larger bodies of the institution, it helps to have a broad basis for appeal.

The best student appeals are those that seek a remedy which instructors, deans, administrators, and others who might be presiding over the appeal can't find on their own. Including potential remedies in the appeal can sometimes help decision makers move toward the position of the student. Advocates often ask students what their "ideal" resolution would be, as well as what they would settle for. For example, a student who has rightfully failed a course, but only by a sliver of a percentage of the total course, might appeal for the chance to redo a single assignment. While there may not normally be grounds for such an appeal, the advocate may cause doubt in the mind of the decision-maker about the instructor's performance, or the situation for the student, or some other aspect of the case. In this way, the advocate may be able to convince the decision-maker to simply allow a single assignment to be redone rather than dealing with the fallout of a failure.

Meetings, Mediation, and Consultation

Depending on the policy of the institution, the student may be required to seek a meeting with their instructor prior to continuing on with the process for the appeal. It is likely that the student has already informally spoken with their instructor about the matter before they've reached out to the students' union office. However, there are rare occurrences where students require assistance with this step. Following this, the formal process will usually then require the student to file the paperwork and meet with the dean or other senior member of the department in which the appeal is taking place. The advocate should participate in all meetings, mediation, and or consultation with the student about the matter as the process continues. Unless there is an opportunity to advance the student's position, the advocate counsels the student simply to take notes to prepare for the steps in the process.

If the student's position is particularly strong, or if the department head or dean that the matter falls under is particularly reasonable, then the matter may be resolved at this stage. From the advocate's position, this is usually the best time to resolve the matter. Deans and department heads have particular flexibility in implementing remedies for students that usually are broader than what will be achieved during an appeal hearing or other formal steps. Building relationships with the deans and department heads can be a fruitful endeavor for student advocates, but should never cross the line of putting student appeals at risk of failure for the sake of maintaining relationships.

Hearings

Student appeals may proceed to a hearing process. The advocate should compile all of the information about the case, keep notes about the process, and prepare the student for next steps. It is important to prepare to advocate directly for the student in the hearing process. The format for hearings varies greatly from institution to institution, but will likely include a chair, as well as student and faculty representatives, all of whom will deliberate on the matter. This is particularly true of academic appeals, though behavioral and other sorts of appeals may have greatly different structures.

In most hearings, the student and or the advocate will be able to provide an overview of the matter at hand, the argument for the student's position, and suggested remedies for the matter. In the case of an academic appeal the instructor may be called upon to provide their perspective of events. It is important for the advocate to determine the sympathies of the hearing committee early on, and adapt the argument to win them over. This is particularly important in programs or courses that are technical, as it is difficult to convince faculty involved in technical professions that a student might be in the right despite the judgment of their instructor, particularly within healthcare faculties.

CHANGING INSTITUTIONAL POLICY

By institutionalizing advocacy for members, a students' union can elevate the effectiveness of both individual student advocacy and of the students' union's campaigns for education reform. Gathering information about student appeals as they happen, engaging in research about appeals and grievance procedures in other institutions and situations, and compiling that research into documents and documentation that can be used for lobbying afterward in campaign efforts is a natural extension of the advocate's position.

Research

A significant wealth of research exists about principles of fairness, winning grievances in various situations, and other aspects of advocacy. The students' union is in a unique position to engage in research about students' issues at the institution. Advocates should be required to collect information about appeals, while maintaining members' confidentiality, for the betterment of the membership. This could include information that will assist in the short-term and long-term improvement of the educational environment.

Over the course of their work, an advocate will encounter some issues on a recurring basis. For example, there may be a department or instructor related to an unusually high number of appeals. Identifying issues with instructors, departments, or other divisions of the institution can be the first step in alleviating the issue. This work should include collecting, identifying, and documenting matters related to gender, sexual orientation, race, ethnicity, culture, and religion across the institution. Any ongoing trends within the institution that impact students' ability to receive an education, and are cause for student appeals on an ongoing basis, should be included in this research.

By building a relationship with the institution's administrators responsible for oversight, an advocate can share their research about student issues. Often, institutional human resource employees, ombudspeople, student affairs professionals, and others within the institution will have experience that will be of benefit to students. Additionally, unions on campus that represent academic and non-academic workers will engage in any number of grievances for their members. There may be overlap in the source of some of these grievances, and grounds to work together to improve the institution for all.

Policy

Lobbying for the development of new policy for the post-secondary institution, and ensuring that it is implemented fairly and strictly, is important for the student advocate. The natural progression of engaging in student advocacy and collecting research about it is to ensure that that research is used to improve the post-secondary institution. Where time allows, advocates should be appointed to the institution's committees that relate to the development of policy in this area. If the institution is slow moving to improve education conditions based on significant recommendations, the students' union should consider its options including but not limited to engaging in political campaigns for reform.

MOVING FORWARD

Answering the question of "where do we go from here" is something that all student organizers must do for their unique set of circumstances. The conditions on each campus are different, as are students' readiness to participate in political action. Developing a collective of students who are knowledgeable and enthusiastic about action is a first step. From the collective will comes democratic direction for a platform of reforms, a campaign strategy, and building connections within the campus community.

In a general sense, there are some changes that must be championed across Canada for students to have unity in action and strive for common goals. These changes include uniting students better at the provincial and cross-Canada level, developing campaigns that are effective to win reforms for students, and building an understanding among students about these goals. Each of these changes will develop in unison, not one after the other. The complicated nature of students' unionism in Canada, given the campus-to-campus, province-to-province nature of students' unions makes this shift challenging, but not impossible. All of this work starts at the local level within campus collectives and local students' unions.

Fostering Collectivism

Among student organizers, the difficult work of fostering collectivism should be a priority. The dominant ideology of capitalism, from the time of childhood until a student reaches campus, instills the perspective that individual self-interest is of utmost importance. The "greed-is-good ideology" of capitalism is toxic to student organizing and to building solidarity. Students are only on campus for the few short years that they are studying, making it difficult to implement long-term ideological change. This means that developing an understanding of the importance of collective work and collective action is a continuous part of student organizing.

Combating liberalism on campus is a part of fostering collectivism. This means developing collectives of students who hold themselves responsible for the work of their organizations, leveraging small collectives to develop campaigns on campus, and fighting for progressive direction in students' unions. Organizers must hold themselves and their collective responsible for the lot of students on campus. For example, if a year goes by on campus where no work is done among the students on that campus to fight to reduce tuition fees, then it is just as much the fault of organizers on that campus as it is of the government increasing tuition fees. Only through building a general understanding of this, and holding each other accountable, can a truly militant student movement be developed.

New Perspectives on Students' Union Organizing

For decades, the student movement has focused on mobilizing a small portion of the membership to achieve its goals. This strategy is a failure, as it has not produced the results required to significantly advance objective conditions for students or the ultimate goals of the student movement.

In her work, and her book *No Shortcuts: Organising for Power in the New Gilded Age*, experienced American trade unionist Jane McAlevey stresses the importance of rallying "whole worker" majorities for the labour movement. The basis for this sort of organizing is a holistic approach to the lives of workers, at work and in the community, and what is needed to advance their lot. Not only does McAlevey call for majority support for the actions of the labour movement among workers, but majority participation as well. Democracy is seen not as a mail-in rebate on union membership, but as an expenditure of time and effort for common goals.

There is no reason that students' unions cannot approach organizing in a more holistic way, as described by McAlevey. Students' union leadership, collectively on campus and between institutions, must reflect on the position of post-secondary students in Canadian society and the ultimate goals of the movement. Rooting objectives in the ultimate goals of the movement and engaging in majority organizing is essential to significant advancements in the position of students and workers.

Mass Action and Solidarity

The demand for high-quality universally accessible public post-secondary education, the central goal of the student movement in Canada, is rooted in strengthening the position of the working class. The very wealthy don't care if tuition fees go up (or down, with the exception of paying more taxes) because it's no real issue for them to pay the fees. Making education more accessible is about making education more accessible for working people.

One area of critical concern for the common struggle of students and workers is the organizational capacity of both. The labour movement has lost ground in recent decades, with a lower percentage overall of working people being members of unions. Statistics Canada estimates that roughly 29 percent of workers were unionized in 2014. Students depend on the labour movement to function effectively for the emancipation of working people from the tyranny of capitalism. From time to time, students' unions can assist the unionization of works, particularly on campus. However, the best way for students to invest in the success of working people's struggle for political power is by building a strong student movement.

APPENDIX I

NOTE ON THE HISTORY OF PAN-CANADIAN STUDENT ORGANIZATIONS

Knowing about the history of the student movement in Canada will inform the work of building more effective campaigns on campus. When students' unionists don't have some understanding of the history of the movement, time is wasted on reinventing goals, strategy, and tactics. Only by having a fulsome understanding of how the movement has evolved can the mistakes of the past be avoided and the successes be repeated.

Early Years

Post-secondary education in Canada pre-dates Confederation. These institutions were mostly reserved for wealthy white men. Since the establishment of universities at that time, there have been organizations to represent students in Canada. The earliest student organizations existed as social clubs that sometimes provided services to students, such as bulk purchasing of sports equipment.

In 1926, the National Federation of Canadian University Students (NFCUS) was formed. At the time, Canada remained a dominion of the British Empire, and earlier in that year, the Imperial Debate Team brought organizers of the United Kingdom's National Union of Students across the Atlantic. These organizers encouraged students' Student Administrative Councils, then the name for many students' societies, to form a Canadian equivalent to the National Union of Students.

The National Federation of Canadian University Students was founded to provide student services, enable communication between students, and advocate for improved post-secondary education curriculum and policy. Included in the founding goals was lobbying for reduced transportation tariffs for students and student groups

Financial concerns dominated the conferences of the NFCUS because there was often not enough money collected from students to fund its projects. After only a few years, annual conferences were scrapped in favour of bi-annual conferences. Membership in international student groups was always a challenge because of low revenue.

Expansion of Student Population

The NFCUS was dormant during World War II. After the war, veterans began to demand access to college and university education for themselves and their children. This expanding population changed the demographics of student populations and began to change the demographics of students' society leadership.

In 1947, the NFCUS membership was divided over its participation in the International Union of Students. The IUS membership included many communist student organizations, including that of the Soviet Union, which was a source of concern for some NFCUS members. Conditional membership was sought in the IUS for a two-year period, but conditional membership was refused by IUS members as undemocratic.

Starting in the late 1940s, the NFCUS began to lobby for increased funding for post-secondary education. During the first half of the

1950s, the organization made presentations to government, including the Prime Minister, about creating student financial assistance programs.

Decades of Activism

Internal debates and conflicts led various students' societies to disaffiliate and re-affiliate during the 1950s and 1960s. At one point, students from Quebec urged the organization not to lobby government for student financial aid and a decision was made in their favour in the interest of maintaining membership numbers. Despite this, in 1964, Quebec students formed their own national student organization. By this time, the National Federation of Canadian University Students changed its name to Canadian Union of Students, partially because of the establishment of numerous colleges across Canada.

The Canadian Union of Students then sought new and expansive student financial assistance programs. In 1968 the organization passed a controversial motion condemning United States of America in their aggression and warmongering in Vietnam, causing students from some schools to disaffiliate.

During the 1960s and 1970s, provincial students' unions began to develop. These organizations, including the Ontario Federation of Students and British Columbia Students' Federation, advocated for increased funding for post-secondary education. At times, provincial students' unions organized students to pressure governments for reductions or the elimination of tuition fees.

In 1972, after the decline of the Canadian Union of Students, the National Union of Students was founded. The NUS brought provincial students' unions together, acting as a framework for communication between various organizations. However, membership in the NUS never reached near comprehensive numbers of Canadian post-secondary students, and the organization was limited by a lack of funds.

For many involved in the NUS, the 1970s were a period of organizational "building." NUS reports reflect this perspective, including calling for a new organizational framework with stable finances and widespread support. In 1981 the National Union of Students and the Association of Student Councils, a service-focused organization, merged to form the Canadian Federation of Students.

Canadian Federation of Students

In 1993, the Federal Liberal government threatened to introduce income-contingent student loan repayment. This form of loan repayment would ensure that low-income student loan holders pay vastly more interest than their high-income counterparts. Essentially, the scheme would exacerbate student loans as a tax on lower-income Canadians. The resulting demonstrations, organized by the CFS, were some of the largest in the history of the country.

The early 1990s also saw the emergence of the Canadian Alliance of Student Associations. This group, formed by former members and local students' unions that had long rivaled the CFS, never sought to mass mobilize students for accessible education. Individual students have no say in their students' union's membership in CASA, and rarely does the organization involve rank and file students in its efforts. The group's membership declined over the 2010s.

Through lobbying and membership mobilization, the Canadian Federation of Students saw one of its largest successes in 2010 with the establishment of the Canadian Student Grant Program. The program, a demand of the student movement since the 1960s, was implemented along the suggestion of the CFS down to its name. Despite lower than requested funding, the program represented a significant material improvement in the lives of hundreds of thousands of working-class Canadians.

In 2012, the CFS held a national day of action calling for a federal post-secondary act. The day of action drew tens of thousands to demonstrations across the country, but failed to pressure the federal Conservative Government to take meaningful action.

After a period of slight growth in the early 2000s, the Canadian Federation of Students began a slow and painful membership decline. From 2013 to 2015, the National Executive allowed every affiliated students' union from Quebec to leave through either legal negotiation or unopposed referendum. In 2015, students in British Columbia began to distance themselves from the CFS by changing their provincial students' union's name from Canadian Federation of Students-British Columbia to British Columbia Federation of Students.

APPENDIX II

GLOSSARY OF RELEVANT TERMS

Knowing what these terms, phrases, and acronyms mean will serve student organizers well.

Agitation

Literature or other messaging that evokes an emotional response from the viewer. This is meant to draw them in for a larger conversation.

Board of Governors

The committee of government appointees, elected students, and elected employees that make financial and other governance decisions about a post-secondary institution. One half of the bicameral post-secondary governance system.

British Columbia Federation of Students

Formerly the British Columbia Students' Federation, then the Canadian Federation of Students-British Columbia, the British Columbia Federation of Students (BCFS) is a provincial student organization in British Columbia.

Campaign

A combination of goals, strategy, and tactics that are implemented to reach a desired objective.

Canadian Federation of Students

Founded in 1981, a pan-Canadian student organization with two branches, one focused on reform and the other on services. Also has provincial affiliates.

Collective

A cooperative enterprise that relies on the dedication of its participating individuals to succeed. Collectives derive an added value from dividing cumbersome or numerous tasks amongst participants.

Fiduciary

A person who has a legal position of trust with an individual or organization. In the context of students' unions, directors a have fiduciary duty to the organization.

Grassroots

Grassroots can mean anything from simply the membership of an organization, to an organizing style that shuns structure and centralization. Often used as juxtaposition to the establishment or leadership of a movement. Sometimes used to describe mobilization done without the explicit sanction of a group such as a labour union, student organization, or political party.

Individualism

Valuing the whims of the individual above all else. In a political sense, this is referred to as liberalism.

Liberalism

In the context of social movements, liberalism or "Small 'L' Liberalism" is the tendency of putting one's own success before the success of the movement.

Majority

A majority is half of an assembly, group, or democratic body, plus one. Often referred to as "50 percent, plus one". Basic democracy empowers a majority to make decisions to take action, as long as those decisions respect the rights of participants, minority position holders, and absentees.

Member

All individuals who meet the membership requirements of a students' union, as defined by the constitution and bylaws.

Minority

A minority is half or less of an assembly, group, or democratic body. Minority positions are not empowered to decide on actions. In students' unions, minority position holders are protected by rules of order, organizational policy, and law.

Oppression

The state of being subject to undue control and/or manipulation.

Petition

A list of supporters collected to demonstrate the support for an idea or cause. In modern political campaigns, petitions are commonly used as a method to collect supporters' contact information.

Public Interest Research Group (PIRG)

Public Interest Research Groups, originally formed in the United States of America in place of students' unions, are student membership organizations that engage in social justice causes.

Senate

A committee of elected faculty, students, and academic staff that governs curriculum, academic planning, and program standards. At colleges, this body is referred to as the Education Council. One half of the bicameral post-secondary governance system.

Tuition

Tuition, often referred to as "tuition fees" to emphasize that it is a fee, is a tax on education. Tuition is a user fee, meaning only those who use the service pay the tax.

SELECTED BIBLIOGRAPHY

Bond, Becky, and Exley, Zack. *Rules for Revolutionaries: How Big Organizing Can Change Everything*. Chelsea Green, White River Junction. 2016.

Bradbury, Alexandra, et al. *How to Jump-Start Your Union: Lessons from the Chicago Teachers*. Labor Notes, Detroit. 2015.

Dimitrov, Georgi. "The United Workers' Front." *Selected Works*. Sofia Press, Sofia. 1972. Volume 1.

Lenin, Vladimir. "The Student Movement and the Present Political Situation". *Proletary*, No. 36, October 3 (16), 1908. Lenin Collected Works, Progress Publishers, 1973, Moscow, Volume 15, pages 213-219.

Lopez, Lori Kido. "A Media Campaign For Ourselves: Building Organizational Media Capacity Through Participatory Action Research." *Journal Of Media Practice* 16.3 (2015): 228-244.

McAlevey, Jane. *No Shortcuts: Organizing for Power in the New Gilded Age*. Oxford University Press, New York. 2016.

Min, Qiu, et al. "Employees' Psychological Ownership And Self-Efficacy As Mediators Between Performance Appraisal Purpose And Proactive Behavior." *Social Behavior & Personality: An International Journal* 43.7 (2015): 1101-1109.

Oedy, Bob. *Bigger Labor: A Crash Course for Construction Union Organisers*. Union Organiser Press, Winnetka. 2008.

Pronin, I. and Stepichev, M. *Leninist Standards of Party Life*. Progress Publishers, Moscow. 1969.

Skills Development Weekend Resource Manual. British Columbia Federation of Students. Vancouver. 2016.

ABOUT THE AUTHOR

Zachary Crispin is the Executive Director of the Selkirk College Students' Union. He has served in various elected roles, representing students across British Columbia and Canada.

Zachary Crispin can be reached at:
Selkirk College Students' Union
Room 0-127, 301 Frank Beinder Way
Castlegar, BC, V1N 4L3
E-mail: z.crispin@selkirkstudents.ca